Paper anniversary pr

PENGUI

PENGUIN'S POEMS FOR LIFE

LAURA BARBER is former editorial director for Penguin Classics and now publishes contemporary literature. She lives in London.

Penguin's Poems *for* Life

Selected with a preface by
LAURA BARBER

PENGUIN BOOKS

PENGUIN CLASSICS

Published by the Penguin Group
Penguin Books Ltd, 80 Strand, London WC2R ORL, England
Penguin Group (USA) Inc., 375 Hudson Street, New York, New York 10014, USA
Penguin Group (Canada), 90 Eglinton Avenue East, Suite 700, Toronto, Ontario, Canada M4P 2Y3
(a division of Pearson Penguin Canada Inc.)
Penguin Ireland, 25 St Stephen's Green, Dublin 2, Ireland (a division of Penguin Books Ltd)
Penguin Group (Australia), 250 Camberwell Road, Camberwell, Victoria 3124, Australia
(a division of Pearson Australia Group Pty Ltd)
Penguin Books India Pvt Ltd, 11 Community Centre, Panchsheel Park, New Delhi – 110 017, India
Penguin Group (NZ), 67 Apollo Drive, Rosedale, North Shore 0632, New Zealand
(a division of Pearson New Zealand Ltd)
Penguin Books (South Africa) (Pty) Ltd, 24 Sturdee Avenue, Rosebank, Johannesburg 2196, South Africa

Penguin Books Ltd, Registered Offices: 80 Strand, London WC2R ORL, England

www.penguin.com

First published 2007
Published in paperback in Penguin Classics 2008
8

Selection and editorial material copyright © Laura Barber, 2007
All rights reserved

The moral right of the editor has been asserted

The Acknowledgements on pages 368–75 constitute an extension of this copyright page

Typeset by Rowland Phototypesetting Ltd, Bury St Edmunds, Suffolk
Printed in England by Clays Ltd, St Ives plc

ISBN: 978-0-140-42470-6

www.greenpenguin.co.uk

Penguin Books is committed to a sustainable future
for our business, our readers and our planet.
The book in your hands is made from paper
certified by the Forest Stewardship Council.

Contents

Childhood and Childish Things

Growing Up and First Impressions

Making a Living and Making Love

Family Life, for Better, for Worse

Getting Older, Looking Back

Intimations of Mortality

Mourning and Monuments

JAQUES:

                      All the world's a stage,
And all the men and women merely players:
They have their exits and their entrances;
And one man in his time plays many parts,
His acts being seven ages. At first the infant,
Mewling and puking in the nurse's arms.
And then the whining school-boy, with his satchel
And shining morning face, creeping like snail
Unwillingly to school. And then the lover,
Sighing like furnace, with a woeful ballad
Made to his mistress' eyebrow. Then a soldier,
Full of strange oaths and bearded like the pard,
Jealous in honour, sudden and quick in quarrel,
Seeking the bubble reputation
Even in the cannon's mouth. And then the justice,
In fair round belly with good capon lined,
With eyes severe and beard of formal cut,
Full of wise saws and modern instances;
And so he plays his part. The sixth age shifts
Into the lean and slipper'd pantaloon,
With spectacles on nose and pouch on side,
His youthful hose, well saved, a world too wide
For his shrunk shank; and his big manly voice,
Turning again toward childish treble, pipes
And whistles in his sound. Last scene of all,
That ends this strange eventful history,
Is second childishness and mere oblivion,
Sans teeth, sans eyes, sans taste, sans everything.

    William Shakespeare, *As You Like It*, II, vii

Preface

'I need a poem.' This may not be a sentence you expect to come across very often in your life, but since beginning to think about this book, it's one I've heard a lot: from friends who are planning their weddings or trying to find the right thing to say at a funeral, and from others who are stuck for words while writing a birthday card or find themselves in need of distraction when they arrive at work on a drizzly Monday morning. The effect of a well-chosen poem can be real and tangible – it can soothe a bruised heart, patch a broken friendship, lull a baby to sleep, seduce the hesitant or console the bereaved. And while most of us probably don't read poetry every single day, it seems that there are plenty of times in our lives when only a poem will do. This is a book that sets out to meet that need, by offering a selection of poems to accompany you through life, from birth to death, and a little beyond.

The structure of the book was inspired by a few lines in Shakespeare's play *As You Like It*, in which one of the characters, Jacques, describes a human life as having seven distinct ages. The images he conjures up for each age are broadly familiar to us today, but these lines also reveal as much about the misanthropic nature of the character who uttered them (the sullen Jacques is known as 'Monsieur Melancholy') as about the human life cycle itself. In thinking about how poetry might trace a modern lifeline, I wanted this anthology to be shaped less by how the different phases of life might look from the outside (still less to a cynical outsider) than by how they feel from the inside – whether experienced, remembered or imagined. And if, in the spirit of the contrarian Queen in *Alice's Adventures in Wonderland*, who declared herself capable of believing 'six impossible things before breakfast', we experience ourselves as having several possible sides to our personalities at any given time (perhaps especially before breakfast), we will also want poems that constantly push beyond this notion of playing a series of discrete roles in life determined by our age, and instead express the complexity and endless variety of what it means to be alive and human.

We start off then with birth and babies and the mysterious beginnings of existence, before moving into childhood and the tottering first steps towards an awareness of who we are and what else the world contains. The section on growing up brings us an intoxicating taste of independence, and explores the dizzying possibilities on offer – in life and in love. The next stage looks at the practical reality of making our way in adult life – through the dogged persistence of routine at work, and the equally dogged pursuit of relaxation and romance. The chapter on family life covers the whole range of experiences we might find in loving and living with other people, before we turn to the poems about growing older, whether this hurls us towards a flamboyant midlife crisis or we relish the slower pace of life. In the seventh part we are brought face to face with the prospect of death and travel right up to life's closing moments. At this point the book takes us beyond Shakespeare's 'seven ages', with the addition of an extra section devoted to the experience of living on after the end of someone else's life, and the strange journey of grief from the initial shock of loss towards a time when the agony of absence might be replaced by the sense of a continued, though different, presence.

Within these eight sections, the poems are not organized by when or where they were written, but by what they say. As well as speaking to the various themes of each stage of life, this allows the poems to speak to each other too, sometimes as a deliberate response to an earlier work and sometimes in conversations that are unintended and unexpected. Of course, any anthology that departs from the neutrality of chronology, geography or the alphabet as a way of arranging itself necessarily introduces a more singular and subjective order and, like Jacques's, the lifeline that this book maps out is inevitably a personal one, but not – I hope – prescriptive. If you read continuously, each part tells its own story about a different period of life, but you can also approach a single section like a lucky dip, rummaging about until you find the poem that perfectly matches your mood or picking one out at random and allowing yourself to be transported somewhere unexpected.

Here you will find some of the best-loved poems from the past, poems whose words resonate as richly today as they did when they were first written, and whose sentiments still seem as true. The well-known lines of these poems seem now to be woven into the very fabric of our culture, the threads running so deep that some of the ways we understand or think about life seem to follow the pattern laid out by an earlier word-perfect expression. There are also contemporary voices in English from around the world, questioning the traditional ways of seeing life, re-imagining the limits to what we can feel or be, and making modern music out of today's ever-evolving language. Old or new, what these poems share is an ability to rise to the challenge of finding the right words. We may believe with Wordsworth that poets should avoid fancy phrases in favour of 'language really used by men', but the reason we sometimes turn to a poem rather than look for our own words is that our 'real' use of language can be haphazard and hasty, and a good poem happens when a poet has found a way – and taken the time – to use our language more precisely and carefully than we tend to. A poem may allow us to say what we really mean in another sense too, especially when we are dealing with occasions or events that don't occur every day. Poetry does not shy away from significant moments or milestones, and it is not afraid of confronting the raw or awkward facts of life, sex and death. At such times, poetry may be able to say more than we feel able to articulate: it can speak more honestly than a close friend, more passionately than a cautious lover, more bravely than an embarrassed stranger.

As well as the public occasions like births, marriages or funerals, I also wanted to include some poems for the more private rites of passage or emotional crossroads – when you realize that a sibling has grown up and left you behind or that you need to disentangle yourself from a flailing relationship; when you experience the nervous exhilaration of your first kiss or admit the guilty exhaustion of looking after children; when you are struggling to emerge from the black depths of depression or find yourself reeling from a sudden, fresh stab of loss. And then there are poems that describe the less intense incidents of daily life – the white lie you tell your child, the grey hair you spot in the mirror, the back-to-school feeling that settles in the pit of your stomach on a Sunday evening, the drowsy boredom of a slow afternoon in the office, the bitter marital bickering that poisons a dinner party, or the comfort of entering a house and knowing that you're home.

Whatever the occasion, poetry is able to capture the moments and emotions of life – even the mundane or ugly ones – and transform them into something remarkable and beautiful. Coleridge defined this potent magic quite simply as 'poetry = the best words in the best order' and a good poem often has the curious effect of describing your state of mind or heart so accurately that it seems instantly recognizable and true, while also startling you with the sensation that you are seeing something familiar as if for the very first time. Such poems enter your imagination, like wine swirling through water, altering the colour and the flavour of your experience.

When we are young, we are quite used to the startling and stirring effect of poetry. It has a natural and instinctive place in our life: as we learn nursery rhymes and join in with playground chants, our enjoyment of poetry is almost physical – we taste the shape of the words in our mouth, we feel the rhythms, and we hear the rhymes. Discovering the right poem at the right time when you are older can be equally powerful and visceral. As Emily Dickinson said: 'If I read a book and it makes my whole body so cold no fire can ever warm me, I know *that* is poetry. If I feel physically as if the top of my head were taken off, I know *that* is poetry.' The encounter may not always be comfortable but, like a good friend, a collection of poems should offer shocks and surprises as well as support; it should shake you out of your usual way of thinking, force you to look at the things you would rather not see, and encourage you to broaden your experience of life by sometimes considering it inside out or upside down. Thomas Gray described poetry as 'thoughts that breathe and words that burn' and, as well as giving expression to our innermost feelings, poems can occasionally push us up against the flames and change us for ever. Whether breathing, or burning, or taking the top of your head off, these are the words that sing in your heart when you hear them and that dance back into your mind years later; they are the lines that somehow become part of your very being and that carry you through your life.

A Note on the Poems

All the poems included here were written in English, but beyond this my aim has been to range as widely as possible – through time and space. The earliest poems in the selection were composed in the fourteenth century and the most recent has only just appeared in print; and the poets themselves come from all parts of the world, including Africa, the Caribbean, India, North and South America, Canada, Europe, the British Isles and the Republic of Ireland.

For ease of comprehension, older poems have been lightly modernized in punctuation and spelling but in the few instances when modernization or standardization would completely alter the feel of the original or amount to translation (the Medieval English and dialect poems), glosses have been provided instead. Where a definitive text has been established by editors (for example, Emily Dickinson and Wilfred Owen) and for all modern works, the poems are reproduced exactly as published.

Birth and
Beginnings

SYLVIA PLATH

Morning Song

Love set you going like a fat gold watch.
The midwife slapped your footsoles, and your bald cry
Took its place among the elements.

Our voices echo, magnifying your arrival. New statue.
In a drafty museum, your nakedness
Shadows our safety. We stand round blankly as walls.

I'm no more your mother
Than the cloud that distills a mirror to reflect its own slow
Effacement at the wind's hand.

All night your moth-breath
Flickers among the flat pink roses. I wake to listen:
A far sea moves in my ear.

One cry, and I stumble from bed, cow-heavy and floral
In my Victorian nightgown.
Your mouth opens clean as a cat's. The window square

Whitens and swallows its dull stars. And now you try
Your handful of notes;
The clear vowels rise like balloons.

WILLIAM BLAKE

Infant Sorrow

My mother groan'd, my father wept,
Into the dangerous world I leapt;
Helpless, naked, piping loud,
Like a fiend hid in a cloud.

Struggling in my father's hands,
Striving against my swaddling-bands,
Bound and weary, I thought best
To sulk upon my mother's breast.

WALTER DE LA MARE

The Birthnight: To F.

Dearest, it was a night
That in its darkness rocked Orion's stars;
A sighing wind ran faintly white
Along the willows, and the cedar boughs
Laid their wide hands in stealthy peace across
The starry silence of their antique moss:
No sound save rushing air
Cold, yet all sweet with Spring,
And in thy mother's arms, couched weeping there,
        Thou, lovely thing.

THOMAS TRAHERNE

The Salutation

These little Limbs,
These Eyes and Hands which here I find.
These rosy Cheeks wherewith my Life begins,
Where have ye been? Behind
What Curtain were ye from me hid so long?
Where was, in what Abyss, my speaking Tongue?

When silent I,
So many thousand, thousand years
Beneath the Dust did in a Chaos lie,
How could I Smiles or Tears,
Or Lips or Hands or Eyes or Ears perceive?
Welcome ye Treasures which I now receive.

I that so long
Was Nothing from Eternity,
Did little think such Joys as Ear or Tongue
To celebrate or see:
Such Sounds to hear, such Hands to feel, such Feet,
Beneath the Skies, on such a Ground to meet.

New burnished Joys!
Which yellow Gold and Pearls excel!
Such sacred Treasures are the Limbs in Boys,
In which a Soul doth Dwell;
Their organized Joints and azure Veins
More Wealth include than all the World contains.

From Dust I rise,
And out of Nothing now awake;
These brighter Regions which salute mine Eyes,
A Gift from God I take.
The Earth, the Seas, the Light, the Day, the Skies,
The Sun and Stars are mine, if those I prize.

Long time before
I in my mother's Womb was born,
A God preparing did this Glorious Store,
The World, for me adorn.
Into this Eden so divine and fair,
So wide and bright, I come His Son and Heir.

A Stranger here
Strange Things doth meet, strange Glories see;
Strange Treasures lodg'd in this fair World appear,
Strange all, and new to me;
But that they mine should be, who nothing was,
That Strangest is of all, yet brought to pass.

ANNE STEVENSON

The Spirit is too Blunt an Instrument

The spirit is too blunt an instrument
to have made this baby.
Nothing so unskilful as human passions
could have managed the intricate
exacting particulars: the tiny
blind bones with their manipulating tendons,
the knee and the knucklebones, the resilient
fine meshings of ganglia and vertebrae
in the chain of the difficult spine.

Observe the distinct eyelashes and sharp crescent
fingernails, the shell-like complexity
of the ear with its firm involutions
concentric in miniature to the minute
ossicles. Imagine the
infinitesimal capillaries, the flawless connections
of the lungs, the invisible neural filaments
through which the completed body
already answers to the brain.

Then name any passion or sentiment
possessed of the simplest accuracy.
No. No desire or affection could have done
with practice what habit
has done perfectly, indifferently,
through the body's ignorant precision.
It is left to the vagaries of the mind to invent
love and despair and anxiety
and their pain.

ALFRED, LORD TENNYSON

Little bosom not yet cold,
Noble forehead made for thought,
Little hands of mighty mould
Clenched as in the fight which they had fought.
He had done battle to be born,
But some brute force of Nature had prevailed
And the little warrior failed.
Whate'er thou wert, whate'er thou art,
Whose life was ended ere thy breath begun,
Thou nine-months neighbour of my dear one's heart,
And howsoe'er thou liest blind and mute,
Thou lookest bold and resolute,
God bless thee dearest son.

E. E. CUMMINGS

from spiralling ecstatically this

proud nowhere of earth's most prodigious night
blossoms a newborn babe:around him,eyes
– gifted with every keener appetite
than mere unmiracle can quite appease –
humbly in their imagined bodies kneel
(over time space doom dream while floats the whole

perhapsless mystery of paradise)

mind without soul may blast some universe
to might have been,and stop ten thousand stars
but not one heartbeat of this child;nor shall
even prevail a million questionings
against the silence of his mother's smile

– whose only secret all creation sings

ANONYMOUS

from the *Chester Cycle of the Mystery Plays*

The Creation

DEUS:
> I, God, most in maiestye,
> In whom beginning none may be,
> Endles as most of postye,
> I am and have bene ever.
> Now heaven and earth is made through me:
> The earthe is voyde onely I see,
> Therefore light for more lee,
> Through my crafte I will kever.

> At my bydding now made be light!
> Light is good, I see in sighte;
> Twynned shalbe throughe my mighte
> The lighte from thesternes.
> Light daye I will be called aye,
> And thesternes night, as I say;
> Thus morrow and even the first day
> Is made full and expresse.

> Now will I make the fyrmament
> In myddes the waters to be lent,
> For to be a divident,
> To twyne the waters aye;
> Above the welkin, benethe also,
> And heaven yt shall be called oo;
> Thus commen is even and morrow also
> Of the seacond daye.

postye power; *lee* brightness; *kever* gain; *Twynned* divided; *thesternes* darkness; *aye* ever; *expresse* complete; *fyrmament* sky; *myddes* midst; *lent* placed; *welkin* sky; *oo* always; *even* evening

Now will I waters everichone,
That under heaven be great won,
That they [gather] into one,
And drynes sone him showe.
That drynes earth men shall call;
The gathering of the waters all,
Seas to name have the shall,
Thereby men shall [them] knowe.

I will on earth that hearbes springe,
Each one in kinde seede gevinge,
Trees dyvers fruytes forth bringe,
After there kinde eache one,
The seede of which for aye shall be
Within the fruyte of each tree;
Thus morrow and even of dayes three
Is bothe comen and gone.

Now will I make through my might
Lightninge in the welken brighte,
To twyn the day from the nighte,
And lighten the earthe with lee.
Greate lightes also I will make twoo,
The sonne and eke the mone also;
The sonne for daye to serve for oo,
The mone for nighte to be.

I will make on the fyrmament
Starres also, throughe myne intent;
The earth to lighten there they be sent,
And knowne may be there-bye
Cowrses of planetts nothing amisse.
Now se I this worke good, i-wisse;
Thus morrow and even both made is
The fourthe daye fully.

won existence; *sone* soon; *hearbes* plants; *kinde* nature; *dyvers* diverse; *Cowrses* courses; *i-wisse* indeed

Now will I in waters fishe forth bringe,
Fowles in the firmament flyinge,
Great whalles in the sea swymminge;
All make I with a thoughte.
Beastes, fowles, stone and tree,
These workes are good, well I see,
Therfore to blesse all lykes me
These workes that I have wroughte.

All beastes I byd yow multeply
In earth, in water, by and bye,
And fowles in ayre for to flye
The earth to fulfill.
Thus morrow and even, through my might,
Of the fifte daye and the night
Is made and ended well arighte,
All at myne owne will.

Now will I on earth forth bringe anone
All kindes of beastes, everichon,
That creepen, flye, or els gone,
Each one in his kinde.
Now is done all my biddinge,
Beastes going, flyinge and creeping,
And all my workes at my lyking
Fully now I finde.

Now heaven and earth is made expresse,
Make we man to our lyckenes;
Fishe, foule, beastes, more and lesse
To maister he shall have might.
To our shape now make I thee;
Man and woman I will ther be.
Growe and multeply shall ye
And fulfill earth in height.

lykes pleases

To helpe thee, thou shalt have here
Hearbes, trees, sede, fruite in feare;
All shalbe put in thy power,
And beastes eke also,
All that in earth be sterring,
Fowles in the ayer flying,
And all that ghoste hath and lyking,
To sustayne yow from woe.

Now this is done, I see aright,
And all thinges made through my might,
The sixte daye here in my sight
Is made all of the beste.
Heaven and earth is wrought within,
And all that needes to be therin;
To-morrow, the seventh day, I will blyn,
And of worke take my reste.

feare company; *sterring* stirring; *ayer* air; *ghoste* spirit; *blyn* stop

W. S. MERWIN

Just This

When I think of the patience I have had
back in the dark before I remember
or knew it was night until the light came
all at once at the speed it was born to
with all the time in the world to fly through
not concerned about ever arriving
and then the gathering of the first stars
unhurried in their flowering spaces
and far into the story the planets
cooling slowly and the ages of rain
then the seas starting to bear memory
the gaze of the first cell at its waking
how did this haste begin this little time
at any time this reading by lightning
scarcely a word this nothing this heaven

from *Pleasant Comedy of Patient Grissil,* IV, ii

Golden slumbers kiss your eyes,
Smiles awake you when you rise.
Sleep, pretty wantons, do not cry,
And I will sing a lullaby:
Rock them, rock them, lullaby.

Care is heavy, therefore sleep you,
You are care and care must keep you.
Sleep, pretty wantons, do not cry,
And I will sing a lullaby:
Rock them, rock them, lullaby.

SAMUEL TAYLOR COLERIDGE

Frost at Midnight

The Frost performs its secret ministry,
Unhelped by any wind. The owlet's cry
Came loud – and hark, again! loud as before.
The inmates of my cottage, all at rest,
Have left me to that solitude, which suits
Abstruser musings: save that at my side
My cradled infant slumbers peacefully.
'Tis calm indeed! so calm, that it disturbs
And vexes meditation with its strange
And extreme silentness. Sea, hill, and wood,
This populous village! Sea, and hill, and wood,
With all the numberless goings-on of life,
Inaudible as dreams! the thin blue flame
Lies on my low-burnt fire, and quivers not;
Only that film, which fluttered on the grate,
Still flutters there, the sole unquiet thing.
Methinks, its motion in this hush of nature
Gives it dim sympathies with me who live,
Making it a companionable form,
Whose puny flaps and freaks the idling Spirit
By its own moods interprets, every where
Echo or mirror seeking of itself,
And makes a toy of Thought.

                              But O! how oft,
How oft, at school, with most believing mind,
Presageful, have I gazed upon the bars,
To watch that fluttering *stranger*! and as oft
With unclosed lids, already had I dreamt
Of my sweet birth-place, and the old church-tower,
Whose bells, the poor man's only music, rang
From morn to evening, all the hot Fair-day,
So sweetly, that they stirred and haunted me

With a wild pleasure, falling on mine ear
Most like articulate sounds of things to come!
So gazed I, till the soothing things, I dreamt,
Lulled me to sleep, and sleep prolonged my dreams!
And so I brooded all the following morn,
Awed by the stern preceptor's face, mine eye
Fixed with mock study on my swimming book:
Save if the door half opened, and I snatched
A hasty glance, and still my heart leaped up,
For still I hoped to see the *stranger's* face,
Townsman, or aunt, or sister more beloved,
My play-mate when we both were clothed alike!

    Dear Babe, that sleepest cradled by my side,
Whose gentle breathings, heard in this deep calm,
Fill up the interspersèd vacancies
And momentary pauses of the thought!
My babe so beautiful! it thrills my heart
With tender gladness, thus to look at thee,
And think that thou shalt learn far other lore,
And in far other scenes! For I was reared
In the great city, pent 'mid cloisters dim,
And saw nought lovely but the sky and stars.
But *thou*, my babe! shalt wander like a breeze
By lakes and sandy shores, beneath the crags
Of ancient mountain, and beneath the clouds,
Which image in their bulk both lakes and shores
And mountain crags: so shalt thou see and hear
The lovely shapes and sounds intelligible
Of that eternal language, which thy God
Utters, who from eternity doth teach
Himself in all, and all things in himself.
Great universal Teacher! he shall mould
Thy spirit, and by giving make it ask.

    Therefore all seasons shall be
Whether the summer clothe
With greenness, or the re
Betwixt the tufts of s

Of mossy apple-tree, while the nigh thatch
Smokes in the sun-thaw; whether the eave-drops fall
Heard only in the trances of the blast,
Or if the secret ministry of frost
Shall hang them up in silent icicles,
Quietly shining to the quiet Moon.

WALT WHITMAN

A Noiseless Patient Spider

A noiseless patient spider,
I mark'd where on a little promontory it stood isolated,
Mark'd how to explore the vacant vast surrounding,
It launch'd forth filament, filament, filament, out of itself,
Ever unreeling them, ever tirelessly speeding them.

And you O my soul where you stand,
Surrounded, detached, in measureless oceans of space,
Ceaselessly musing, venturing, throwing, seeking the
    spheres to connect them,
Till the bridge you will need be form'd, till the ductile
    anchor hold,
Till the gossamer thread you fling catch somewhere,
    O my soul.

SYLVIA PLATH

You're

Clownlike, happiest on your hands,
Feet to the stars, and moon-skulled,
Gilled like a fish. A common-sense
Thumbs-down on the dodo's mode.
Wrapped up in yourself like a spool,
Trawling your dark as owls do.
Mute as a turnip from the Fourth
Of July to All Fools' Day,
O high-riser, my little loaf.

Vague as fog and looked for like mail.
Farther off than Australia.
Bent-backed Atlas, our traveled prawn.
Snug as a bud and at home
Like a sprat in a pickle jug.
A creel of eels, all ripples.
Jumpy as a Mexican bean.
Right, like a well-done sum.
A clean slate, with your own face on.

PERCY BYSSHE SHELLEY

To Ianthe

I love thee, Baby! for thine own sweet sake:
Those azure eyes, that faintly dimpled cheek,
Thy tender frame so eloquently weak,
Love in the sternest heart of hate might wake;
But more, when o'er thy fitful slumber bending
Thy mother folds thee to her wakeful heart,
Whilst love and pity in her glances blending,
All that thy passive eyes can feel, impart;
More, when some feeble lineaments of her
Who bore thy weight beneath her spotless bosom,
As with deep love I read thy face, recur,
More dear art thou, O fair and fragile blossom,
Dearest, when most thy tender traits express
The image of thy Mother's loveliness. –

THOMAS HARDY

Heredity

I am the family face;
Flesh perishes, I live on,
Projecting trait and trace
Through time to times anon,
And leaping from place to place
Over oblivion.

The years-heired feature that can
In curve and voice and eye
Despise the human span
Of durance – that is I;
The eternal thing in man,
That heeds no call to die.

AMBROSE PHILIPS

To Miss Charlotte Pulteney, in her mother's arms

Timely blossom, infant fair,
Fondling of a happy pair,
Every morn, and every night
Their solicitous delight,
Sleeping, waking, still at ease,
Pleasing, without skill to please;
Little gossip, blithe and hale,
Tattling many a broken tale,
Singing many a tuneless song,
Lavish of a heedless tongue;
Simple maiden, void of art,
Babbling out the very heart,
Yet abandon'd to thy will,
Yet imagining no ill,
Yet too innocent to blush,
Like the linnet in the bush
To the mother-linnet's note
Moduling her slender throat;
Chirping forth thy pretty joys,
Wanton in the change of toys,
Like the linnet green, in May,
Flitting to each bloomy spray;
Wearied then, and glad of rest,
Like the linnet in the nest.
This thy present happy lot
This, in time, will be forgot:
Other pleasures, other cares,
Ever-busy time prepares;
And thou shalt in thy daughter see,
This picture, once, resembled thee.

CHINUA ACHEBE

Generation Gap

A son's arrival
is the crescent moon
too new too soon to lodge
the man's returning. His
feast of reincarnation
must await the moon's
ripening at the naming
ceremony of his
grandson.

ELIZABETH BARRETT BROWNING

from *Aurora Leigh*, Sixth Book

                              There he lay upon his back,
The yearling creature, warm and moist with life
To the bottom of his dimples, – to the ends
Of the lovely tumbled curls about his face;
For since he had been covered over-much
To keep him from the light-glare, both his cheeks
Were hot and scarlet as the first live rose
The shepherd's heart-blood ebbed away into,
The faster for his love. And love was here
As instant! in the pretty baby-mouth,
Shut close as if for dreaming that it sucked;
The little naked feet drawn up the way
Of nestled birdlings; everything so soft
And tender, – to the little holdfast hands,
Which, closing on a finger into sleep,
Had kept the mould of't.
                              While we stood there dumb,
For oh, that it should take such innocence
To prove just guilt, I thought, and stood there dumb;
The light upon his eyelids pricked them wide,
And, staring out at us with all their blue,
As half perplexed between the angelhood
He had been away to visit in his sleep,
And our most mortal presence, – gradually
He saw his mother's face, accepting it
In change for heaven itself, with such a smile
As might have well been learnt there, – never moved,
But smiled on, in a drowse of ecstasy,
So happy (half with her and half with heaven)
He could not have the trouble to be stirred,
But smiled and lay there. Like a rose, I said:

As red and still indeed as any rose,
That blows in all the silence of its leaves,
Content in blowing to fulfil its life.

She leaned above him (drinking him as wine)
In that extremity of love, 'twill pass
For agony or rapture, seeing that love
Includes the whole of nature, rounding it
To love . . . no more, – since more can never be
Than just love. Self-forgot, cast out of self,
And drowning in the transport of the sight,
Her whole pale passionate face, mouth, forehead, eyes,
One gaze, she stood! then, slowly as he smiled
She smiled too, slowly, smiling unaware,
And drawing from his countenance to hers
A fainter red, as if she watched a flame
And stood in it a-glow. 'How beautiful,'
Said she.

GERARD MANLEY HOPKINS

Spring

Nothing is so beautiful as Spring –
    When weeds, in wheels, shoot long and lovely and lush;
    Thrush's eggs look little low heavens, and thrush
Through the echoing timber does so rinse and wring
The ear, it strikes like lightnings to hear him sing;
    The glassy peartree leaves and blooms, they brush
    The descending blue; that blue is all in a rush
With richness; the racing lambs too have fair their fling.

What is all this juice and all this joy?
    A strain of the earth's sweet being in the beginning
In Eden garden. – Have, get, before it cloy,
    Before it cloud, Christ, lord, and sour with sinning,
Innocent mind and Mayday in girl and boy,
    Most, O maid's child, thy choice and worthy the
        winning.

WILLIAM BLAKE

The Angel that presided o'er my birth
Said 'Little creature, form'd of joy and mirth,
Go, love without the help of anything on earth.'

Childhood and
Childish Things

HENRY VAUGHAN

The Retreat

Happy those early days, when I
Shined in my angel infancy!
Before I understood this place
Appointed for my second race,
Or taught my soul to fancy aught
But a white, celestial thought,
When yet I had not walked above
A mile, or two, from my first love,
And looking back (at that short space)
Could see a glimpse of his bright face;
When on some gilded cloud, or flow'r
My gazing soul would dwell an hour,
And in those weaker glories spy
Some shadows of eternity;
Before I taught my tongue to wound
My conscience with a sinful sound,
Or had the black art to dispense
A sev'ral sin to ev'ry sense,
But felt through all this fleshly dress
Bright shoots of everlastingness.
    Oh how I long to travel back
And tread again that ancient track!
That I might once more reach that plain
Where first I left my glorious train,
From whence th' enlightened spirit sees
That shady city of palm trees;
But (ah!) my soul with too much stay
Is drunk, and staggers in the way.
Some men a forward motion love,
But I by backward steps would move,
And when this dust falls to the urn
In that state I came return.

WILLIAM WORDSWORTH

Ode (Intimations of Immortality from Recollections of Early Childhood)

Paulò majora canamus

There was a time when meadow, grove, and stream,
The earth, and every common sight,
   To me did seem
   Apparelled in celestial light,
The glory and the freshness of a dream.
It is not now as it has been of yore; –
   Turn wheresoe'er I may,
   By night or day,
The things which I have seen I now can see no more.

   The Rainbow comes and goes,
   And lovely is the Rose,
   The Moon doth with delight
  Look round her when the heavens are bare;
   Waters on a starry night
   Are beautiful and fair;
  The sunshine is a glorious birth;
  But yet I know, where'er I go,
That there hath passed away a glory from the earth.

Now, while the Birds thus sing a joyous song,
   And while the young Lambs bound
   As to the tabor's sound,
To me alone there came a thought of grief:
A timely utterance gave that thought relief,
   And I again am strong.
The Cataracts blow their trumpets from the steep,
No more shall grief of mine the season wrong;
I hear the Echoes through the mountains throng,
The Winds come to me from the fields of sleep,

And all the earth is gay,
        Land and sea
Give themselves up to jollity,
        And with the heart of May
Doth every Beast keep holiday,
        Thou Child of Joy,
Shout round me, let me hear thy shouts, thou happy
    Shepherd Boy!

Ye blessed Creatures, I have heard the call
        Ye to each other make; I see
The heavens laugh with you in your jubilee;
        My heart is at your festival,
        My head hath its coronal,
The fullness of your bliss, I feel – I feel it all.
            Oh evil day! if I were sullen
            While the Earth herself is adorning,
                This sweet May-morning,
            And the Children are pulling,
                On every side,
            In a thousand valleys far and wide,
            Fresh flowers; while the sun shines warm,
And the Babe leaps up on his mother's arm: –
        I hear, I hear, with joy I hear!
        – But there's a Tree, of many one,
A single Field which I have looked upon,
Both of them speak of something that is gone:
            The Pansy at my feet
            Doth the same tale repeat:
Whither is fled the visionary gleam?
Where is it now, the glory and the dream?

Our birth is but a sleep and a forgetting:
The Soul that rises with us, our life's Star,
        Hath had elsewhere its setting,
            And cometh from afar:
        Not in entire forgetfulness,
        And not in utter nakedness,

But trailing clouds of glory do we come
              From God, who is our home:
Heaven lies about us in our infancy!
Shades of the prison-house begin to close
              Upon the growing Boy,
But He beholds the light, and whence it flows,
              He sees it in his joy;
The Youth, who daily farther from the East
        Must travel, still is Nature's Priest,
              And by the vision splendid
              Is on his way attended;
At length the Man perceives it die away,
And fade into the light of common day.

Earth fills her lap with pleasures of her own;
Yearnings she hath in her own natural kind,
And, even with something of a Mother's mind,
              And no unworthy aim,
        The homely Nurse doth all she can
To make her Foster-child, her Inmate Man,
              Forget the glories he hath known,
And that imperial palace whence he came.

Behold the Child among his new-born blisses,
A four year's Darling of a pigmy size!
See, where mid work of his own hand he lies,
Fretted by sallies of his Mother's kisses,
With light upon him from his Father's eyes!
See, at his feet, some little plan or chart,
Some fragment from his dream of human life,
Shaped by himself with newly-learned art;
              A wedding or a festival,
              A mourning or a funeral;
                  And this hath now his heart,
                  And unto this he frames his song:
                  Then will he fit his tongue
To dialogues of business, love, or strife;
              But it will not be long

Ere this be thrown aside,
        And with new joy and pride
The little Actor cons another part,
Filling from time to time his 'humorous stage'
With all the Persons, down to palsied Age,
That Life brings with her in her Equipage;
        As if his whole vocation
        Were endless imitation.

Thou, whose exterior semblance doth belie
        Thy Soul's immensity;
Thou best Philosopher, who yet dost keep
Thy heritage, thou Eye among the blind,
That, deaf and silent, read'st the eternal deep,
Haunted for ever by the eternal mind, –
        Mighty Prophet! Seer blest!
        On whom those truths do rest,
Which we are toiling all our lives to find,
In darkness lost, the darkness of the grave;
Thou, over whom thy Immortality
Broods like the Day, a Master o'er a Slave,
A Presence which is not to be put by;
        To whom the grave
Is but a lonely bed without the sense or sight
        Of day or the warm light,
A place of thought where we in waiting lie;
Thou little Child, yet glorious in the might
Of untamed pleasures, on thy Being's height,
Why with such earnest pains dost thou provoke
The Years to bring the inevitable yoke,
Thus blindly with thy blessedness at strife?
Full soon thy Soul shall have her earthly freight,
And custom lie upon thee with a weight,
Heavy as frost, and deep almost as life!

        O joy! that in our embers
        Is something that doth live,
        That nature yet remembers
        What was so fugitive!

The thought of our past years in me doth breed
Perpetual benedictions: not indeed
For that which is most worthy to be blest;
Delight and liberty, the simple creed
Of Childhood, whether fluttering or at rest,
With new-born hope for ever in his breast: –
              Not for these I raise
           The song of thanks and praise;
        But for those obstinate questionings
           Of sense and outward things,
           Fallings from us, vanishings;
           Blank misgivings of a Creature
Moving about in worlds not realized,
High instincts, before which our mortal Nature
Did tremble like a guilty Thing surprized:
        But for those first affections,
        Those shadowy recollections,
           Which, be they what they may,
Are yet the fountain light of all our day,
Are yet a master light of all our seeing;
           Uphold us, cherish us, and make
Our noisy years seem moments in the being
Of the eternal Silence: truths that wake,
              To perish never;
Which neither listlessness, nor mad endeavour,
              Nor Man nor Boy,
Nor all that is at enmity with joy,
Can utterly abolish or destroy!
        Hence, in a season of calm weather,
           Though inland far we be,
Our Souls have sight of that immortal sea
           Which brought us hither,
           Can in a moment travel thither,
And see the Children sport upon the shore,
And hear the mighty waters rolling evermore.

Then, sing ye Birds, sing, sing a joyous song!
           And let the young Lambs bound
           As to the tabor's sound!

We in thought will join your throng,
  Ye that pipe and ye that play,
  Ye that through your hearts to day
  Feel the gladness of the May!
What though the radiance which was once so bright
Be now for ever taken from my sight,
  Though nothing can bring back the hour
Of splendour in the grass, of glory in the flower;
  We will grieve not, rather find
  Strength in what remains behind,
  In the primal sympathy
  Which having been must ever be,
  In the soothing thoughts that spring
  Out of human suffering,
  In the faith that looks through death,
In years that bring the philosophic mind.

And oh ye Fountains, Meadows, Hills, and Groves,
Think not of any severing of our loves!
Yet in my heart of hearts I feel your might;
I only have relinquished one delight
To live beneath your more habitual sway.
I love the Brooks which down their channels fret,
Even more than when I tripped lightly as they;
The innocent brightness of a new-born Day
   Is lovely yet;
The Clouds that gather round the setting sun
Do take a sober colouring from an eye
That hath kept watch o'er man's mortality;
Another race hath been, and other palms are won.
Thanks to the human heart by which we live,
Thanks to its tenderness, its joys, and fears,
To me the meanest flower that blows can give
Thoughts that do often lie too deep for tears.

R. S. THOMAS

Children's Song

We live in our own world.
A world that is too small
For you to stoop and enter
Even on hands and knees,
The adult subterfuge.
And though you probe and pry
With analytic eye,
And eavesdrop all our talk
With an amused look,
You cannot find the centre
Where we dance, where we play,
Where life is still asleep
Under the closed flower,
Under the smooth shell
Of eggs in the cupped nest
That mock the faded blue
Of your remoter heaven.

TED HUGHES

Full Moon and Little Frieda

A cool small evening shrunk to a dog bark
    and the clank of a bucket –
And you listening.
A spider's web, tense for the dew's touch.
A pail lifted, still and brimming – mirror
To tempt a first star to a tremor.

Cows are going home in the lane there, looping the
    hedges with their warm wreaths of breath –
A dark river of blood, many boulders,
Balancing unspilled milk.

'Moon!' you cry suddenly, 'Moon! Moon!'

The moon has stepped back like an artist gazing
    amazed at a work

That points at him amazed

ROBERT LOUIS STEVENSON

Escape at Bedtime

The lights from the parlour and kitchen shone out
   Through the blinds and the windows and bars;
And high overhead and all moving about,
   There were thousands of millions of stars.
There ne'er were such thousands of leaves on a tree,
   Nor of people in church or the Park,
As the crowds of the stars that looked down upon me,
   And that glittered and winked in the dark.

The Dog, and the Plough, and the Hunter, and all,
   And the star of the sailor, and Mars,
These shone in the sky, and the pail by the wall
   Would be half full of water and stars.
They saw me at last, and they chased me with cries,
   And they soon had me packed into bed;
But the glory kept shining and bright in my eyes,
   And the stars going round in my head.

EUGENE FIELD

Dutch Lullaby

Wynken, Blynken, and Nod one night
   Sailed off in a wooden shoe, –
Sailed on a river of misty light
   Into a sea of dew.
'Where are you going, and what do you wish?'
   The old moon asked the three.
'We have come to fish for the herring-fish
   That live in this beautiful sea;
   Nets of silver and gold have we,'
         Said Wynken,
         Blynken,
         And Nod.

The old moon laughed and sung a song,
   As they rocked in the wooden shoe;
And the wind that sped them all night long
   Ruffled the waves of dew;
The little stars were the herring-fish
   That lived in the beautiful sea.
'Now cast your nets wherever you wish,
   But never afeard are we!'
   So cried the stars to the fishermen three,
         Wynken,
         Blynken,
         And Nod.

All night long their nets they threw
   For the fish in the twinkling foam,
Then down from the sky came the wooden shoe,
   Bringing the fishermen home;

'T was all so pretty a sail, it seemed
　　As if it could not be;
And some folk thought 't was a dream they'd
　　　　　　dreamed
　　Of sailing that beautiful sea;
　　But I shall name you the fishermen three:
　　　　　　Wynken,
　　　　　　Blynken,
　　　　　　And Nod.

Wynken and Blynken are two little eyes,
　　And Nod is a little head,
And the wooden shoe that sailed the skies
　　Is a wee one's trundle-bed;
So shut your eyes while Mother sings
　　Of wonderful sights that be,
And you shall see the beautiful things
　　As you rock on the misty sea
　　Where the old shoe rocked the fishermen three, –
　　　　　　Wynken,
　　　　　　Blynken,
　　　　　　And Nod.

WALT WHITMAN

There Was a Child Went Forth

There was a child went forth every day,
And the first object he look'd upon, that object he became,
And that object became part of him for the day or a certain part
    of the day,
Or for many years or stretching cycles of years.

The early lilacs became part of this child,
And grass and white and red morning-glories, and white and red
    clover, and the song of the phoebe-bird,
And the Third-month lambs and the sow's pink-faint litter, and
    the mare's foal and the cow's calf,
And the noisy brood of the barnyard or by the mire of the
    pond-side,
And the fish suspending themselves so curiously below there, and
    the beautiful curious liquid,
And the water-plants with their graceful flat heads, all became
    part of him.

The field-sprouts of Fourth-month and Fifth-month became part
    of him,
Winter-grain sprouts and those of the light-yellow corn, and the
    esculent roots of the garden,
And the apple-trees cover'd with blossoms and the fruit
    afterward, and wood-berries and the commonest weeds by
    the road,
And the old drunkard staggering home from the outhouse of the
    tavern whence he had lately risen,
And the schoolmistress that pass'd on her way to the school,
And the friendly boys that pass'd, and the quarrelsome boys,
And the tidy and fresh-cheek'd girls, and the barefoot negro boy
    and girl,
And all the changes of city and country wherever he went.

His own parents, he that had father'd him and she that had
   conceiv'd him in her womb and birth'd him,
They gave this child more of themselves than that,
They gave him afterward every day, they became part of him.
The mother at home quietly placing the dishes on the
   supper-table,
The mother with mild words, clean her cap and gown, a
   wholesome odor falling off her person and clothes as she
   walks by,
The father, strong, self-sufficient, manly, mean, anger'd, unjust,
The blow, the quick loud word, the tight bargain, the crafty lure,
The family usages, the language, the company, the furniture, the
   yearning and swelling heart,
Affection that will not be gainsay'd, the sense of what is real, the
   thoughts if after all it should prove unreal,
The doubts of day-time and the doubts of night-time, the curious
   whether and how,
Whether that which appears so is so, or is it all flashes and
   specks?
Men and women crowding fast in the streets, if they are not
   flashes and specks what are they?
The streets themselves and the façades of houses, and goods in
   the windows,
Vehicles, teams, the heavy-plank'd wharves, the huge crossing at
   the ferries,
The village on the highland seen from afar at sunset, the river
   between,
Shadows, aureola and mist, the light falling on roofs and gables
   of white or brown two miles off,
The schooner near by sleepily dropping down the tide, the little
   boat slack-tow'd astern,
The hurrying tumbling waves, quick-broken crests, slapping,
The strata of color'd clouds, the long bar of maroon-tint away
   solitary by itself, the spread of purity it lies motionless in,
The horizon's edge, the flying sea-crow, the fragrance of salt
   marsh and shore mud,
These became part of that child who went forth every day, and
   who now goes, and will always go forth every day.

ANONYMOUS

What are little boys made of?
  Frogs and snails
  And puppy-dogs' tails,
That's what little boys are made of.

What are little girls made of?
  Sugar and spice
  And all things nice,
That's what little girls are made of.

ANONYMOUS

There was a little girl, who had a little curl,
  Right in the middle of her forehead;
When she was good, she was very, very good,
  But when she was bad, she was horrid.

LEWIS CARROLL

from *Alice Through the Looking-Glass*

Jabberwocky

'Twas brillig, and the slithy toves
  Did gyre and gimble in the wabe;
All mimsy were the borogoves,
    And the mome raths outgrabe.

'Beware the Jabberwock, my son!
  The jaws that bite, the claws that catch!
Beware the Jubjub bird, and shun
    The frumious Bandersnatch!'

He took his vorpal sword in hand:
  Long time the manxome foe he sought –
So rested he by the Tumtum tree,
    And stood awhile in thought.

And as in uffish thought he stood,
  The Jabberwock, with eyes of flame,
Came whiffling through the tulgey wood,
    And burbled as it came!

One, two! One, two! And through and through
  The vorpal blade went snicker-snack!
He left it dead, and with its head
    He went galumphing back.

'And hast thou slain the Jabberwock?
  Come to my arms, my beamish boy!
O frabjous day! Callooh! Callay!'
    He chortled in his joy.

'Twas brillig, and
Did gyre and gimbl
All mimsy were the borog
And the mome raths out

THOMAS MORE

Childhood

I am called Childhood, in play is all my mind,
To cast a coyte, a cokstele, and a ball.
A top can I set, and drive it in his kind.
But would to god these hateful books all,
Were in a fire burnt to powder small.
Than might I lead my life always in play:
Which life god send me to mine ending day.

he slithy toves
in the wabe;
oves,
rabe.

o,
w.

hree,
Me.

s Four,
I was not much more.

When I was Five,
I was just alive.

But now I am Six, I'm as clever as clever.
So I think I'll be six now for ever and ever.

WINTHROP MACKWORTH PRAED

Childhood and His Visitors

Once on a time, when sunny May
   Was kissing up the April showers,
I saw fair Childhood hard at play
   Upon a bank of blushing flowers;
Happy, – he knew not whence or how;
   And smiling, – who could choose but love him?
For not more glad than Childhood's brow,
   Was the blue heaven that beamed above him.

Old Time, in most appalling wrath,
   That valley's green repose invaded;
The brooks grew dry upon his path,
   The birds were mute, the lilies faded;
But Time so swiftly winged his flight,
   In haste a Grecian tomb to batter,
That Childhood watched his paper kite,
   And knew just nothing of the matter.

With curling lip, and glancing eye,
   Guilt gazed upon the scene a minute,
But Childhood's glance of purity
   Had such a holy spell within it,
That the dark demon to the air
   Spread forth again his baffled pinion,
And hid his envy and despair,
   Self-tortured, in his own dominion.

Then stepped a gloomy phantom up,
   Pale, cypress-crowned, Night's awful daughter,
And proffered him a fearful cup,
   Full to the brim of bitter water:

Poor Childhood bade her tell her name,
　　And when the beldame muttered 'Sorrow',
He said, – 'don't interrupt my game,
　　I'll taste it, if I must, to-morrow.'

The Muse of Pindus thither came,
　　And wooed him with the softest numbers
That ever scattered wealth and fame
　　Upon a youthful poet's slumbers;
Though sweet the music of the lay,
　　To Childhood it was all a riddle,
And 'Oh,' he cried, 'do send away
　　That noisy woman with the fiddle.'

Then Wisdom stole his bat and ball,
　　And taught him, with most sage endeavour,
Why bubbles rise, and acorns fall,
　　And why no toy may last for ever:
She talked of all the wondrous laws
　　Which Nature's open book discloses,
And Childhood, ere she made a pause,
　　Was fast asleep among the roses.

Sleep on, sleep on! – Oh! Manhood's dreams
　　Are all of earthly pain, or pleasure,
Of Glory's toils, Ambition's schemes,
　　Of cherished love, or hoarded treasure:
But to the couch where Childhood lies
　　A more delicious trance is given,
Lit up by rays from Seraph eyes,
　　And glimpses of remembered Heaven!

DEREK MAHON

Jardin du Luxembourg

(after Rilke)

A merry-go-round of freshly painted horses
sprung from a childish world vividly bright
before dispersing in adult oblivion
and losing its quaint legendary light
spins in the shadows of a burbling circus.
Some draw toy coaches but remain upright;
a roebuck flashes past, a fierce red lion
and every time an elephant ivory-white.

As if down in the forest of Fontainebleau
a little girl wrapped up in royal blue
rides round on a unicorn; a valiant son
hangs on to the lion with a frantic laugh,
hot fists gripping the handles for dear life;
then that white elephant with ivory tusks –
an intense scrum of scarves and rumpled socks
though the great whirligig is just for fun.

The ring revolves until the time runs out,
squealing excitedly to the final shout
as pop-eyed children gasp there in their grey
jackets and skirts, wild bobble and beret.
Now you can study faces, different types,
the tiny features starting to take shape
with proud, heroic grins for the grown-ups,
shining and blind as if from a mad scrape.

Children

When folk come on, as summer burns,
    O'er flower-bloomings, year by year,
To men and women in their turns,
    And strive in hope, or toil in fear,
And their sweet children come to show
    Before them, each its pretty face,
How friends come, one by one, to know
    Whom most they match, of all their race.

'Oh! he is like his sire,' some cry,
    'Cast in his father's very mould,'
Or 'She would fit the very die
    Her mother fitted, just as old;'
Or 'Ah! that boy has uncle's nose,
    Of uncle's shapings more than half,'
Or 'Oh! that smiling baby shows
    Her aunty Polly's merry laugh.'

Thus coming children bring again
    The lines and looks of earlier lives,
The gait and ways of father-men,
    The smile or voice of long gone wives;
And, oh! how well in tune we see
    The copied lines, for ever shown,
Though every coming child shall be
    An unmatch'd self, Himself alone.

SPIKE MILLIGAN

My Sister Laura

My sister Laura's bigger than me
And lifts me up quite easily.
I can't lift her, I've tried and tried;
She must have something heavy inside.

LOUIS UNTERMEYER

Portrait of a Child

Unconscious of amused and tolerant eyes,
He sits among his scattered dreams, and plays,
True to no one thing long; running for praise
With something less than half begun. He tries
To build his blocks against the furthest skies.
They fall; his soldiers tumble; but he stays
And plans and struts and laughs at fresh dismays,
Too confident and busy to be wise.

His toys are towns and temples; his commands
Bring forth vast armies trembling at his nod.
He shapes and shatters with impartial hands.
And, in his crude and tireless play, I see
The savage, the creator, and the god:
All that man was and all he hopes to be.

GEORGE ELIOT

from *Brother and Sister*

I

I cannot choose but think upon the time
When our two lives grew like two buds that kiss
At lightest thrill from the bee's swinging chime,
Because the one so near the other is.

He was the elder and a little man
Of forty inches, bound to show no dread,
And I the girl that puppy-like now ran,
Now lagged behind my brother's larger tread.

I held him wise, and when he talked to me
Of snakes and birds, and which God loved the best,
I thought his knowledge marked the boundary
Where men grew blind, though angels knew the rest.

  If he said 'Hush!' I tried to hold my breath
  Wherever he said 'Come!' I stepped in faith.

OLIVIA MCCANNON

Probability

He always tried to make it better
Put it right
To stop it happening at all was best.

Crossing the road he held her small hand
So tightly
Her knuckles turned white with his stress.

On cliff walks he kept her pressed right in
On the inside
Once she walked through a wasps' nest.

Once she jumped out of an upstairs window
She was fine
She wanted to see what can happen.

SEAMUS HEANEY

The Railway Children

When we climbed the slopes of the cutting
We were eye-level with the white cups
Of the telegraph poles and the sizzling wires.

Like lovely freehand they curved for miles
East and miles west beyond us, sagging
Under their burden of swallows.

We were small and thought we knew nothing
Worth knowing. We thought words travelled the
    wires
In the shiny pouches of raindrops,

Each one seeded full with the light
Of the sky, the gleam of the lines, and ourselves
So infinitesimally scaled

We could stream through the eye of a needle.

JUDITH WRIGHT

Legend

The blacksmith's boy went out with a rifle
and a black dog running behind.
Cobwebs snatched at his feet,
rivers hindered him,
thorn-branches caught at his eyes to make him blind
and the sky turned into an unlucky opal,
but he didn't mind,
I can break branches, I can swim rivers, I can stare
    out any spider I meet,
said he to his dog and his rifle.

The blacksmith's boy went over the paddocks
with his old black hat on his head.
Mountains jumped in his way,
rocks rolled down on him,
and the old crow cried, 'You'll soon be dead.'
And the rain came down like mattocks.
But he only said
I can climb mountains, I can dodge rocks, I can
    shoot an old crow any day,
and he went on over the paddocks.

When he came to the end of the day the sun began
    falling.
Up came the night ready to swallow him,
like the barrel of a gun,
like an old black hat,
like a black dog hungry to follow him.
Then the pigeon, the magpie and the dove began
    wailing
and the grass lay down to pillow him.
His rifle broke, his hat blew away and his dog was gone
and the sun was falling.

But in front of the night the rainbow stood on the
    mountain,
just as his heart foretold.
He ran like a hare,
he climbed like a fox;
he caught it in his hands, the colours and the cold –
like a bar of ice, like the column of a fountain,
like a ring of gold.
The pigeon, the magpie and the dove flew up to stare,
and the grass stood up again on the mountain.

The blacksmith's boy hung the rainbow on his shoulder
instead of his broken gun.
Lizards ran out to see,
snakes made way for him,
and the rainbow shone as brightly as the sun.
All the world said, Nobody is braver, nobody is bolder,
nobody else has done
anything to equal it. He went home as bold as he could be
with the swinging rainbow on his shoulder.

FRANCES CORNFORD

Childhood

I used to think that grown-up people chose
To have stiff backs and wrinkles round their nose,
And veins like small fat snakes on either hand,
On purpose to be grand.
Till through the bannisters I watched one day
My great-aunt Etty's friend who was going away,
And how her onyx beads had come unstrung.
I saw her grope to find them as they rolled;
And then I knew that she was helplessly old,
As I was helplessly young.

ROBERT GRAVES

Warning to Children

Children, if you dare to think
Of the greatness, rareness, muchness,
Fewness of this precious only
Endless world in which you say
You live, you think of things like this:
Blocks of slate enclosing dappled
Red and green, enclosing tawny
Yellow nets, enclosing white
And black acres of dominoes,
Where a neat brown paper parcel
Tempts you to untie the string.
In the parcel a small island,
On the island a large tree,
On the tree a husky fruit.
Strip the husk and pare the rind off:
In the kernel you will see
Blocks of slate enclosed by dappled
Red and green, enclosed by tawny
Yellow nets, enclosed by white
And black acres of dominoes,
Where the same brown paper parcel –
Children, leave the string alone!
For who dares undo the parcel
Finds himself at once inside it,
On the island, in the fruit,
Blocks of slate about his head,
Finds himself enclosed by dappled
Green and red, enclosed by yellow
Tawny nets, enclosed by black
And white acres of dominoes,

With the same brown paper parcel
Still unopened on his knee.
And, if he then should dare to think
Of the fewness, muchness, rareness,
Greatness of this endless only
Precious world in which he says
He lives – he then unties the string.

FELICIA DOROTHEA HEMANS

Casabianca

The boy stood on the burning deck,
  Whence all but he had fled;
The flame that lit the battle's wreck,
  Shone round him o'er the dead.

Yet beautiful and bright he stood,
  As born to rule the storm;
A creature of heroic blood,
  A proud, though child-like form.

The flames roll'd on – he would not go,
  Without his father's word;
That father, faint in death below,
  His voice no longer heard.

He call'd aloud – 'Say, father, say
  If yet my task is done?'
He knew not that the chieftain lay
  Unconscious of his son.

'Speak, Father!' once again he cried,
  'If I may yet be gone!'
– And but the booming shots replied,
  And fast the flames roll'd on.

Upon his brow he felt their breath
  And in his waving hair;
And look'd from that lone post of death,
  In still, yet brave despair.

And shouted but once more aloud,
  'My father! must I stay?'
While o'er him fast, through sail and shroud,
  The wreathing fires made way.

They wrapt the ship in splendor wild,
  They caught the flag on high,
And stream'd above the gallant child,
  Like banners in the sky.

There came a burst of thunder sound –
  The boy – oh! where was he?
– Ask of the winds that far around
  With fragments strew'd the sea!

With mast, and helm, and pennon fair,
  That well had borne their part –
But the noblest thing that perish'd there,
  Was that young faithful heart.

GERARD MANLEY HOPKINS

Spring and Fall

(to a young child)

Márgarét, áre you gríeving
Over Goldengrove unleaving?
Leáves líke the things of man, you
With your fresh thoughts care for, can you?
Ah! ás the heart grows older
It will come to such sights colder
By and by, nor spare a sigh
Though worlds of wanwood leafmeal lie;
And yet you will weep and know why.
Now no matter, child, the name:
Sórrow's spríngs áre the same.
Nor mouth had, no nor mind, expressed
What heart heard of, ghost guessed:
It ís the blight man was born for,
It is Margaret you mourn for.

WILLIAM BLAKE

The School Boy

I love to rise in a summer morn,
When the birds sing on every tree;
The distant huntsman winds his horn,
And the sky-lark sings with me.
O! what sweet company.

But to go to school in a summer morn
O! it drives all joy away;
Under a cruel eye outworn,
The little ones spend the day,
In sighing and dismay.

Ah! then at times I drooping sit,
And spend many an anxious hour.
Nor in my book can I take delight,
Nor sit in learning's bower,
Worn thro' with the dreary shower

How can the bird that is born for joy,
Sit in a cage and sing.
How can a child when fears annoy,
But droop his tender wing,
And forget his youthful spring.

O! father and mother, if buds are nip'd,
And blossoms blown away,
And if the tender plants are strip'd
Of their joy in the springing day,
By sorrow and cares dismay,

How shall the summer arise in joy
Or the summer fruits appear
Or how shall we gather what griefs destroy
Or bless the mellowing year,
When the blasts of winter appear.

JOHN CLARE

Schoolboys in Winter

The schoolboys still their morning rambles take
To neighbouring village school with playing speed,
Loitering with pastime's leisure till they quake,
Oft looking up the wild-geese droves to heed,
Watching the letters which their journeys make;
Or plucking haws on which the fieldfares feed,
And hips, and sloes; and on each shallow lake
Making glib slides, where they like shadows go
Till some fresh pastimes in their minds awake.
Then off they start anew and hasty blow
Their numbed and clumpsing fingers till they glow;
Then races with their shadows wildly run
That stride huge giants o'er the shining snow
In the pale splendour of the winter sun.

THOMAS GRAY

Ode on a Distant Prospect of Eton College

Ye distant spires, ye antique towers,
    That crown the wat'ry glade,
Where grateful Science still adores
    Her Henry's holy Shade;
And ye, that from the stately brow
Of Windsor's heights th' expanse below
    Of grove, of lawn, of mead survey,
Whose turf, whose shade, whose flowers among
Wanders the hoary Thames along
    His silver-winding way:

Ah, happy hills, ah, pleasing shade,
    Ah, fields belov'd in vain,
Where once my careless childhood stray'd,
    A stranger yet to pain!
I feel the gales, that from ye blow,
A momentary bliss bestow,
    As waving fresh their gladsome wing,
My weary soul they seem to sooth,
And, redolent of joy and youth,
    To breathe a second spring.

Say, father Thames, for thou hast seen
    Full many a sprightly race
Disporting on thy margent green
    The paths of pleasure trace,
Who foremost now delight to cleave
With pliant arm thy glassy wave?
    The captive linnet which enthral?
What idle progeny succeed
To chase the rolling circle's speed,
    Or urge the flying ball?

While some on earnest business bent
    Their murm'ring labours ply
'Gainst graver hours, that bring constraint
    To sweeten liberty:
Some bold adventurers disdain
The limits of their little reign,
    And unknown regions dare descry:
Still as they run they look behind,
They hear a voice in every wind,
    And snatch a fearful joy.

Gay hope is theirs by fancy fed,
    Less pleasing when possessed;
The tear forgot as soon as shed,
    The sunshine of the breast:
Theirs buxom health of rosy hue,
Wild wit, invention ever-new,
    And lively cheer of vigour born;
The thoughtless day, the easy night,
The spirits pure, the slumbers light,
    That fly th' approach of morn.

Alas, regardless of their doom
    The little victims play!
No sense have they of ills to come,
    Nor care beyond to-day:
Yet see how all around 'em wait
The Ministers of human fate,
    And black Misfortune's baleful train!
Ah, shew them where in ambush stand
To seize their prey the murd'rous band!
    Ah, tell them, they are men!

These shall the fury Passions tear,
    The vultures of the mind,
Disdainful Anger, pallid Fear,
    And Shame that skulks behind;
Or pining Love shall waste their youth,
Or Jealousy with rankling tooth,

That inly gnaws the secret heart,
And Envy wan, and faded Care,
Grim-visag'd comfortless Despair,
    And Sorrow's piercing dart.

Ambition this shall tempt to rise,
    Then whirl the wretch from high,
To bitter Scorn a sacrifice,
    And grinning Infamy.
The stings of Falsehood those shall try,
And hard Unkindness' alter'd eye,
    That mocks the tear it forc'd to flow;
And keen Remorse with blood defil'd,
And moody Madness laughing wild
    Amid severest woe.

Lo, in the vale of years beneath
    A grisly troop are seen,
The painful family of Death,
    More hideous than their Queen:
This racks the joints, this fires the veins,
That every labouring sinew strains,
    Those in the deeper vitals rage:
Lo, Poverty, to fill the band,
That numbs the soul with icy hand,
    And slow-consuming Age.

To each his suff'rings: all are men,
    Condemn'd alike to groan,
The tender for another's pain;
    Th' unfeeling for his own.
Yet, ah! why should they know their fate?
Since sorrow never comes too late,
    And happiness too swiftly flies,
Thought would destroy their paradise.
No more; where ignorance is bliss,
    'Tis folly to be wise.

GWEN HARWOOD

Father and Child

I   *Barn Owl*

Daybreak: the household slept.
I rose, blessed by the sun.
A horny fiend, I crept
out with my father's gun.
Let him dream of a child
obedient, angel-mild –

old No-Sayer, robbed of power
by sleep. I knew my prize
who swooped home at this hour
with daylight-riddled eyes
to his place on a high beam
in our old stables, to dream

light's useless time away.
I stood, holding my breath,
in urine-scented hay,
master of life and death,
a wisp-haired judge whose law
would punish beak and claw.

My first shot struck. He swayed,
ruined, beating his only
wing, as I watched, afraid
by the fallen gun, a lonely
child who believed death clean
and final, not this obscene

bundle of stuff that dropped,
and dribbled through loose straw
tangling in bowels, and hopped
blindly closer. I saw
those eyes that did not see
mirror my cruelty

while the wrecked thing that could
not bear the light nor hide
hobbled in its own blood.
My father reached my side,
gave me the fallen gun.
'End what you have begun.'

I fired. The blank eyes shone
once into mine, and slept.
I leaned my head upon
my father's arm, and wept,
owl-blind in early sun
for what I had begun.

ALEXANDER POPE

from *An Essay on Criticism*

A little learning is a dang'rous thing;
Drink deep, or taste not the Pierian spring:
There shallow draughts intoxicate the brain,
And drinking largely sobers us again.
Fir'd at first sight with what the Muse imparts,
In fearless youth we tempt the heights of Arts,
While from the bounded level of our mind,
Short views we take, nor see the lengths behind;
But, more advanc'd, behold with strange surprise,
New distant scenes of endless science rise!
So pleas'd at first the tow'ring Alps we try,
Mount o'er the vales, and seem to tread the sky,
Th' eternal snows appear already past,
And the first clouds and mountains seem the last:
But, those attain'd, we tremble to survey
The growing labours of the lengthen'd way,
Th' increasing prospect tires our wand'ring eyes,
Hills peep o'er hills, and Alps on Alps arise!

EDWIN MUIR

Childhood

Long time he lay upon the sunny hill,
  To his father's house below securely bound.
Far off the silent, changing sound was still,
  With the black islands lying thick around.

He saw each separate height, each vaguer hue,
  Where the massed islands rolled in mist away,
And though all ran together in his view
  He knew that unseen straits between them lay.

Often he wondered what new shores were there.
  In thought he saw the still light on the sand,
The shallow water clear in tranquil air,
  And walked through it in joy from strand to strand.

Over the sound a ship so slow would pass
  That in the black hill's gloom it seemed to lie.
The evening sound was smooth like sunken glass,
  And time seemed finished ere the ship passed by.

Grey tiny rocks slept round him where he lay,
  Moveless as they, more still as evening came,
The grasses threw straight shadows far away,
  And from the house his mother called his name.

HUGO WILLIAMS

Scratches

My mother scratched the soles of my shoes
to stop me slipping
when I went away to school.

I didn't think a few scratches
with a pair of scissors
was going to be enough.

I was walking on ice,
my arms stretched out.
I didn't know where I was going.

Her scratches soon disappeared
when I started sliding
down those polished corridors.

I slid into class.
I slid across the hall into the changing-room.
I never slipped up.

I learnt how to skate along with an aeroplane
or a car, looking ordinary,
pretending to have fun.

I learnt how long a run I needed
to carry me as far as the gym
in time for Assembly.

I turned as I went,
my arms stretched out to catch the door jamb
as I went flying past.

PATIENCE AGBABI

North(west)ern

I was twelve as in the 12-bar blues, sick
for the Southeast, marooned on the North Wales coast,
a crotchet, my tongue craving the music
of Welsh, Scouse or Manc; entering the outpost

of Colwyn Bay Pier, midsummer, noon,
niteclub for those of us with the deep ache
of adolescence, when I heard that tune.
Named it in one. Soul. My heart was break

dancing on the road to Wigan Casino,
Northern Soul mecca, where transatlantic bass
beat blacker than blue in glittering mono

then back via Southport, Rhyl to the time, place
I bit the Big Apple. Black. Impatient. Young.
A string of pips exploding on my tongue.

CAROL ANN DUFFY

In Mrs Tilscher's Class

You could travel up the Blue Nile
with your finger, tracing the route
while Mrs Tilscher chanted the scenery.
Tana. Ethiopia. Khartoum. Aswân.
That for an hour, then a skittle of milk
and the chalky Pyramids rubbed into dust.
A window opened with a long pole.
The laugh of a bell swung by a running child.

This was better than home. Enthralling books.
The classroom glowed like a sweet shop.
Sugar paper. Coloured shapes. Brady and Hindley
faded, like the faint, uneasy smudge of a mistake.
Mrs Tilscher loved you. Some mornings, you found
she'd left a good gold star by your name.
The scent of a pencil slowly, carefully, shaved.
A xylophone's nonsense heard from another form.

Over the Easter term, the inky tadpoles changed
from commas into exclamation marks. Three frogs
hopped in the playground, freed by a dunce,
followed by a line of kids, jumping and croaking
away from the lunch queue. A rough boy
told you how you were born. You kicked him, but stared
at your parents, appalled, when you got back home.

That feverish July, the air tasted of electricity.
A tangible alarm made you always untidy, hot,
fractious under the heavy, sexy sky. You asked her
how you were born and Mrs Tilscher smiled,
then turned away. Reports were handed out.
You ran through the gates, impatient to be grown,
as the sky split open into a thunderstorm.

Growing Up
and First
Impressions

C. DAY LEWIS

Walking Away

for Sean

It is eighteen years ago, almost to the day –
A sunny day with the leaves just turning,
The touch-lines new-ruled – since I watched you play
Your first game of football, then, like a satellite
Wrenched from its orbit, go drifting away

Behind a scatter of boys. I can see
You walking away from me towards the school
With the pathos of a half-fledged thing set free
Into a wilderness, the gait of one
Who finds no path where the path should be.

That hesitant figure, eddying away
Like a winged seed loosened from its parent stem,
Has something I never quite grasp to convey
About nature's give-and-take – the small, the scorching
Ordeals which fire one's irresolute clay.

I have had worse partings, but none that so
Gnaws at my mind still. Perhaps it is roughly
Saying what God alone could perfectly show –
How selfhood begins with a walking away,
And love is proved in the letting go.

WILLIAM BARNES

Sister Gone

When Mary on her wedding day,
At last a bride, had gone away
From all her friends that there had spent
The happy day in merriment,
And ringers rang, at evenfall,
Their peals of bells, from great to small,
Within the tower's mossy wall
So high against the evening sky,

Then Jane, that there throughout the day
Had been the gayest of the gay,
At last began to hang her head
And ponder on her sister fled,
And days that seem'd too quickly flown,
To leave her now at home alone,
With no one's life to match her own,
So sad, though hitherto so glad.

It saddened me that moonpaled night
To see her by the wall, in white,
While friends departed mate with mate
Beyond the often-swinging gate,
As there beside the lilac shade,
Where golden-chained laburnum sway'd,
Around her face her hairlocks play'd,
All black with light behind her back.

ANDREW YOUNG

Field-Glasses

Though buds still speak in hints
And frozen ground has set the flints
As fast as precious stones
And birds perch on the boughs, silent as cones,

Suddenly waked from sloth
Young trees put on a ten years' growth
And stones double their size,
Drawn nearer through field-glasses' greater eyes.

Why I borrow their sight
Is not to give small birds a fright
Creeping up close by inches;
I make the trees come, bringing tits and finches.

I lift a field itself
As lightly as I might a shelf,
And the rooks do not rage
Caught for a moment in my crystal cage.

And while I stand and look,
Their private lives an open book,
I feel so privileged
My shoulders prick, as though they were
    half-fledged.

RUDYARD KIPLING

If

If you can keep your head when all about you
    Are losing theirs and blaming it on you,
If you can trust yourself when all men doubt you,
    But make allowance for their doubting too;
If you can wait and not be tired by waiting,
    Or being lied about, don't deal in lies,
Or being hated, don't give way to hating,
    And yet don't look too good, nor talk too wise:

If you can dream – and not make dreams your master;
    If you can think – and not make thoughts your aim;
If you can meet with Triumph and Disaster
    And treat those two impostors just the same;
If you can bear to hear the truth you've spoken
    Twisted by knaves to make a trap for fools,
Or watch the things you gave your life to, broken,
    And stoop and build 'em up with worn-out tools:

If you can make one heap of all your winnings
    And risk it on one turn of pitch-and-toss,
And lose, and start again at your beginnings
    And never breathe a word about your loss;
If you can force your heart and nerve and sinew
    To serve your turn long after they are gone,
And so hold on when there is nothing in you
    Except the Will which says to them: 'Hold on!'

If you can talk with crowds and keep your virtue,
    Or walk with Kings – nor lose the common touch,
If neither foes nor loving friends can hurt you,
    If all men count with you, but none too much;

If you can fill the unforgiving minute
   With sixty seconds' worth of distance run,
Yours is the Earth and everything that's in it,
   And – which is more – you'll be a Man, my son!

LEWIS CARROLL

Rules and Regulations

A short direction
To avoid dejection,
By variations
In occupations,
And prolongation
Of relaxation,
And combinations
Of recreations,
And disputation
On the state of the nation
In adaptation
To your station,
By invitations
To friends and relations,
By evitation
Of amputation,
By permutation,
In conversation,
And deep reflection
You'll avoid dejection.

Learn well your grammar,
And never stammer,
Write well and neatly,
And sing most sweetly,
Be enterprising,
Love early rising,
Go walk of six miles,
Have ready quick smiles,
With lightsome laughter,
Soft flowing after
Drink tea, not coffee;
Never eat toffy.

Eat bread with butter.
Once more, don't stutter.
Don't waste your money,
Abstain from honey.
Shut doors behind you,
(Don't slam them, mind you.)
Drink beer, not porter.
Don't enter the water
Till to swim you are able.
Sit close to the table.
Take care of a candle.
Shut a door by the handle,
Don't push with your shoulder
Until you are older.
Lose not a button.
Refuse cold mutton.
Starve your canaries.
Believe in fairies.
If you are able,
Don't have a stable
With any mangers.
Be rude to strangers.

Moral: Behave.

SAMUEL JOHNSON

A Short Song of Congratulation

Long-expected one and twenty
Ling'ring year, at last is flown,
Pomp and Pleasure, Pride and Plenty
Great Sir John, are all your own.

Loosen'd from the Minor's tether,
Free to mortgage or to sell,
Wild as wind, and light as feather
Bid the slaves of thrift farewell.

Call the Bettys, Kates, and Jennys
Ev'ry name that laughs at Care,
Lavish of your Grandsire's guineas,
Show the Spirit of an heir.

All that prey on vice and folly
Joy to see their quarry fly,
Here the Gamester light and jolly,
There the Lender grave and sly.

Wealth, Sir John, was made to wander,
Let it wander as it will;
See the Jocky, see the Pander,
Bid them come, and take their fill.

When the bonny Blade carouses,
Pockets full, and Spirits high,
What are acres? What are houses?
Only dirt, or wet or dry.

If the Guardian or the Mother
Tell the woes of wilful waste,
Scorn their counsel and their pother,
You can hang or drown at last.

LEMN SISSAY

Going Places

Another
cigarette ash
television serial filled
advert analysing
cupboard starving
front room filling
tea slurping
mind chewing
brain burping
carpet picking
pots watching
room gleaning
toilet flushing
night,
with nothing to do

I think I'll paint roads
on my front room walls
to convince myself
that I'm going places.

WILLIAM SHAKESPEARE

from *Hamlet*, III, i

HAMLET:

    To be, or not to be – that is the question;
    Whether 'tis nobler in the mind to suffer
    The slings and arrows of outrageous fortune
    Or to take arms against a sea of troubles
    And by opposing end them. To die, to sleep –
    No more – and by a sleep to say we end
    The heartache and the thousand natural shocks
    That flesh is heir to. 'Tis a consummation
    Devoutly to be wished. To die, to sleep –
    To sleep – perchance to dream. Ay, there's the rub.
    For in that sleep of death what dreams may come
    When we have shuffled off this mortal coil
    Must give us pause. There's the respect
    That makes calamity of so long life.
    For who would bear the whips and scorns of time,
    Th'oppressor's wrong, the proud man's contumely,
    The pangs of despised love, the law's delay,
    The insolence of office, and the spurns
    That patient merit of th'unworthy takes,
    When he himself might his quietus make
    With a bare bodkin? Who would fardels bear,
    To grunt and sweat under a weary life,
    But that the dread of something after death,
    The undiscovered country, from whose bourn
    No traveller returns, puzzles the will,
    And makes us rather bear those ills we have
    Than fly to others that we know not of?
    Thus conscience does make cowards of us all;
    And thus the native hue of resolution
    Is sicklied o'er with the pale cast of thought,

And enterprises of great pitch and moment
With this regard their currents turn awry
And lose the name of action.

ROBERT FROST

The Road Not Taken

Two roads diverged in a yellow wood,
And sorry I could not travel both
And be one traveler, long I stood
And looked down one as far as I could
To where it bent in the undergrowth;

Then took the other, as just as fair,
And having perhaps the better claim,
Because it was grassy and wanted wear;
Though as for that the passing there
Had worn them really about the same,

And both that morning equally lay
In leaves no step had trodden black.
Oh, I kept the first for another day!
Yet knowing how way leads on to way,
I doubted if I should ever come back.

I shall be telling this with a sigh
Somewhere ages and ages hence:
Two roads diverged in a wood, and I –
I took the one less traveled by,
And that has made all the difference.

THOMAS HARDY

When I set out for Lyonnesse,
    A hundred miles away,
    The rime was on the spray,
And starlight lit my lonesomeness
When I set out for Lyonnesse
    A hundred miles away.

What would bechance at Lyonnesse
    While I should sojourn there
    No prophet durst declare,
Nor did the wisest wizard guess
What would bechance at Lyonnesse
    While I should sojourn there.

When I came back from Lyonnesse
    With magic in my eyes,
    All marked with mute surmise
My radiance rare and fathomless,
When I came back from Lyonnesse
    With magic in my eyes!

JOHN KEATS

On First Looking into Chapman's Homer

Much have I travell'd in the realms of gold,
   And many goodly states and kingdoms seen;
   Round many western islands have I been
Which bards in fealty to Apollo hold.
Oft of one wide expanse had I been told
   That deep-brow'd Homer ruled as his demesne;
   Yet did I never breathe its pure serene
Till I heard Chapman speak out loud and bold:
Then felt I like some watcher of the skies
   When a new planet swims into his ken;
Or like stout Cortez when with eagle eyes
   He star'd at the Pacific – and all his men
Look'd at each other with a wild surmise –
   Silent, upon a peak in Darien.

WILLIAM WORDSWORTH

from *The Prelude*, Book XI (1850)

O pleasant exercise of hope and joy!
For mighty were the auxiliars which then stood
Upon our side, us who were strong in love!
Bliss was it in that dawn to be alive,
But to be young was very Heaven! O times,
In which the meagre, stale, forbidding ways
Of custom, law, and statute, took at once
The attraction of a country in romance!
When Reason seemed the most to assert her rights
When most intent on making of herself
A prime enchantress – to assist the work,
Which then was going forward in her name!
Not favoured spots alone, but the whole Earth,
The beauty wore of promise – that which sets
(As at some moments might not be unfelt
Among the bowers of Paradise itself)
The budding rose above the rose full blown.
What temper at the prospect did not wake
To happiness unthought of? The inert
Were roused, and lively natures rapt away!
They who had fed their childhood upon dreams,
The play-fellows of fancy, who had made
All powers of swiftness, subtilty, and strength
Their ministers, – who in lordly wise had stirred
Among the grandest objects of the sense,
And dealt with whatsoever they found there
As if they had within some lurking right
To wield it; – they, too, who of gentle mood
Had watched all gentle motions, and to these
Had fitted their own thoughts, schemers more mild,
And in the region of their peaceful selves; –
Now was it that *both* found, the meek and lofty
Did both find helpers to their hearts' desire,

And stuff at hand, plastic as they could wish, –
Were called upon to exercise their skill,
Not in Utopia, – subterranean fields, –
Or some secreted island, Heaven knows where!
But in the very world, which is the world
Of all of us, – the place where, in the end,
We find our happiness, or not at all!

EBENEZER JONES

High Summer

I never wholly feel that summer is high,
However green the trees, or loud the birds,
However movelessly eye-winking herds
Stand in field ponds, or under large trees lie,
Till I do climb all cultured pastures by,
That hedged by hedgerows studiously fretted trim,
Smile like a lady's face with lace laced prim,
And on some moor or hill that seeks the sky
Lonely and nakedly, – utterly lie down,
And feel the sunshine throbbing on body and limb,
My drowsy brain in pleasant drunkenness swim,
Each rising thought sink back and dreamily drown,
Smiles creep o'er my face, and smother my lips, and cloy,
Each muscle sink to itself, and separately enjoy.

ROBERT WEVER

In Youth is Pleasure

In a harbour green asleep whereas I lay,
The birds sang sweet in the middes of the day,
I dreamed fast of mirth and play:
    In youth is pleasure, in youth is pleasure.

Methought I walked still to and fro,
And from her company I could not go –
But when I waked it was not so:
    In youth is pleasure, in youth is pleasure.

Therefore my heart is surely plight
Of her alone to have a sight
Which is my joy and heart's delight:
    In youth is pleasure, in youth is pleasure.

ROBERT HERRICK

To the Virgins, to Make Much of Time

Gather ye rose-buds while ye may,
    Old Time is still a flying;
And this same flow'r, that smiles to-day,
    To-morrow will be dying.

The glorious lamp of heav'n, the sun,
    The higher he's a getting;
The sooner will his race be run,
    And nearer he's to setting.

That age is best which is the first,
    When youth and blood are warmer;
But, being spent, the worse; and worst
    Times still succeed the former.

Then be not coy, but use your time;
    And while ye may, go marry:
For, having lost but once your prime,
    You may for ever tarry.

from *Troilus and Criseyde*, Book I

Withinne the temple he wente hym forth pleyinge,
This Troilus, of every wight aboute,
On this lady, and now on that, lokynge,
Wher so she were of town or of withoute;
And upon cas bifel that thorugh a route
His eye percede, and so depe it wente,
Til on Criseyde it smot, and ther it stente.

And sodeynly he wax therwith astoned,
And gan hir bet biholde in thrifty wise.
'O mercy, God,' thoughte he, 'wher hastow woned,
That art so feyr and goodly to devise?'
Therwith his herte gan to sprede and rise,
And softe sighed, lest men myghte hym here,
And caught ayeyn his firste pleyinge chere.

She nas nat with the leste of hire stature,
But alle hire lymes so wel answerynge
Weren to wommanhod, that creature
Was nevere lasse mannyssh in semynge;
And ek the pure wise of hire mevynge
Shewed wel that men myght in hire gesse
Honour, estat, and wommanly noblesse.

---

pleyinge making fun; *wight* person; *wher so* whether; *upon cas bifel* by chance it
happened; *route* crowd; *percede* gazed through; *smot* hit; *stente* stayed; *astoned*
astonished; *hastow* hast thou; *woned* dwelled; *devise* look upon; *caughte ayeyn*
recovered; *pleyinge chere* playful expression; *leste* shortest; *answerynge* corres-
ponding; *semynge* appearance; *pure wise* sheer manner; *mevynge* way of moving;
gesse infer; *estat* dignity

To Troilus right wonder wel with alle
Gan for to like hire mevynge and hire chere,
Which somdel deignous was, for she let falle
Hire look a lite aside in swich manere,
Ascaunces, 'What, may I nat stonden here?'
And after that hir lokynge gan she lighte,
That nevere thoughte hym seen so good a syghte.

And of hire look in him ther gan to quyken
So gret desir and swich affeccioun,
That in his hertes botme gan to stiken
Of hir his fixe and depe impressioun.
And though he erst hadde poured up and down,
He was tho glad his hornes in to shrinke:
Unnethes wiste he how to loke or wynke.

Lo, he that leet hymselven so konnynge,
And scorned hem that Loves peynes dryen,
Was ful unwar that Love hadde his dwellynge
Withinne the subtile stremes of hire yen;
That sodeynly hym thoughte he felte dyen,
Right with hire look, the spirit in his herte –
Blissed be Love, that kan thus folk converte!

somdel deignous somewhat haughty; *Ascaunces* as if to say; *lighte* brighten; *his hertes botme* bottom of his heart; *fixe* unchangeable; *impressioun* image; *erst* before; *poured* stared; *tho* then; *shrinke* draw; *Unnethes* hardly; *wiste* knew; *leet* considered; *konnynge* knowledgeable; *dryen* suffer; *subtile stremes* ethereal beams; *yen* eyes; *dyen* die; Right *just*

JOHN CLARE

First Love

I ne'er was struck before that hour
　　With love so sudden and so sweet
Her face it bloomed like a sweet flower
　　And stole my heart away complete
My face turned pale a deadly pale
　　My legs refused to walk away
And when she looked what could I ail
My life and all seemed turned to clay

And then my blood rushed to my face
　　And took my eyesight quite away
The trees and bushes round the place
　　Seemed midnight at noon day
I could not see a single thing
　　Words from my eyes did start
They spoke as chords do from the string
　　And blood burnt round my heart

Are flowers the winters choice
　　Is love's bed always snow
She seemed to hear my silent voice
　　Not loves appeals to know
I never saw so sweet a face
　　As that I stood before
My heart has left its dwelling place
　　And can return no more –

ROBERT GRAVES

Love Without Hope

Love without hope, as when the young bird-catcher
Swept off his tall hat to the Squire's own daughter,
So let the imprisoned larks escape and fly
Singing about her head, as she rode by.

ELIZABETH DARYUSH

Still-life

Through the open French window the warm sun
lights up the polished breakfast-table, laid
round a bowl of crimson roses, for one –
a service of Worcester porcelain, arrayed
near it a melon, peaches, figs, small hot
rolls in a napkin, fairy rack of toast,
butter in ice, high silver coffee-pot,
and, heaped on a salver, the morning's post.

She comes over the lawn, the young heiress,
from her early walk in her garden-wood
feeling that life's a table set to bless
her delicate desires with all that's good,

that even the unopened future lies
like a love-letter, full of sweet surprise.

APHRA BEHN

from *The Emperor of the Moon*, II, v

When Maidens are young and in their Spring
Of Pleasure, of Pleasure, let 'em take their full Swing,
    full Swing, – full Swing, –
      And Love, and Dance, and Play, and Sing.
     For *Silvia*, believe it, when Youth is done,
There's nought but hum drum, hum drum, hum drum;
There's nought but hum drum, hum drum, hum drum.

Then *Silvia* be wise – be wise – be wise,
Tho' Painting and Dressing, for a while, are Supplies,
    And may – surprise –
      But when the Fire's going out in your Eyes,
     It twinkles, it twinkles, it twinkles, and dies.
And then to hear Love, to hear Love from you,
I'd as lief hear an Owl cry – Wit to woo,
    Wit to woo, Wit to woo.

CHARLES TURNER

A Country Dance

He has not woo'd, but he has lost his heart.
That country dance is a sore test for him;
He thinks her cold; his hopes are faint and dim;
But though with seeming mirth she takes her part
In all the dances, and the laughter there,
And though to many a youth, on brief demand,
She gives a kind assent and courteous hand,
She loves but him, for him is all her care.
With jealous heed her lessening voice he hears
Down that long vista, where she seems to move
Among fond faces and relays of love,
And sweet occasion, full of tender fears:
Down those long lines he watches from above,
Till with the refluent dance she reappears.

KIRSTY GUNN

Mataatua

All the handsome boys from school
rode up front, and crowded there
at the prow of that long canoe. I
remember how we watched them. At night,
we slow-danced with them too. Their hair
was damp; we pressed ourselves
dreaming against their dark jackets like
butterflies in our thin dresses, caught.

GEORGE GORDON, LORD BYRON

from *Don Juan*, Canto I

XC

Young Juan wandered by the glassy brooks
   Thinking unutterable things. He threw
Himself at length within the leafy nooks
   Where the wild branch of the cork forest grew.
There poets find materials for their books,
   And every now and then we read them through,
So that their plan and prosody are eligible,
Unless like Wordsworth they prove unintelligible.

XCI

He, Juan (and not Wordsworth), so pursued
   His self-communion with his own high soul
Until his mighty heart in its great mood
   Had mitigated part, though not the whole
Of its disease. He did the best he could
   With things not very subject to control
And turned, without perceiving his condition,
Like Coleridge into a metaphysician.

XCII

He thought about himself and the whole earth,
   Of man the wonderful and of the stars
And how the deuce they ever could have birth,
   And then he thought of earthquakes and of wars,
How many miles the moon might have in girth,
   Of air balloons and of the many bars
To perfect knowledge of the boundless skies.
And then he thought of Donna Julia's eyes.

In thoughts like these true wisdom may discern
    Longings sublime and aspirations high,
Which some are born with, but the most part learn
    To plague themselves withal, they know not why.
'Twas strange that one so young should thus concern
    His brain about the action of the sky.
If you think 'twas philosophy that this did,
I can't help thinking puberty assisted.

ADRIAN MITCHELL

A Puppy Called Puberty

It was like keeping a puppy in your underpants
A secret puppy you weren't allowed to show to anyone
Not even your best friend or your worst enemy

You wanted to pat him stroke him cuddle him
All the time but you weren't supposed to touch him

He only slept for five minutes at a time
Then he'd suddenly perk up his head
In the middle of school medical inspection
And always on bus rides
So you had to climb down from the upper deck
All bent double to smuggle the puppy off the bus
Without the buxom conductress spotting
Your wicked and ticketless stowaway.

Jumping up, wet-nosed, eagerly wagging –
He only stopped being a nuisance
When you were alone together
Pretending to be doing your homework
But really gazing at each other
Through hot and hazy daydreams

Of those beautiful schoolgirls on the bus
With kittens bouncing in their sweaters.

SASHA DUGDALE

First Love

He asked to see her breasts in the back room of the
    butcher's store.
Silhouetted against the encaustic tiles they rise in points
Childish and disappointing, she thought them,
Insubstantial. Looking down at them,
Departing from the cross arms of her breast bone
Hardly at all. What is it he finds so interesting
She thinks and looks at him, so tirelessly watching
And now stretching out a timid hand, red raw
With cleaving the meat off the hanging carcasses,
Towards her, his hand floats in the air and breathes,
She feels the pulse in his wrist before the touch.
There is no blood on the marble cutting slabs
Nor on the floor, because hygiene is everything
Hygiene is everything, the butcher tells them
When uncooked meat is being handled.
The shop itself is dark. The blue light of the flycatcher
On the wall is all. She buttons up again and leaves him.
He is leaning, eyes closed, up against the door.

TOGARA MUZANENHAMO

Smoke

For a brief moment I was lost in a thought
While walking up the flight of stairs to her room –
Her hand leading me up, my eyes catching a flash
Of her bare thighs under a simple yellow skirt –

And I was a boy again, in that small moment,
Holding a present I had longed and wished for –
Bright blue emotions, sparks in mid-ignition
Bursting in my chest – lights never to grow old.

When I think of her leading me upstairs to her bed,
There's always a thought of that one precious
    Christmas –
The lightweight pig-iron cap-gun, the blind surprise
And spurt of gunpowder-smoke after the first bang.

FREDERICK GODDARD TUCKERMAN

An upper chamber in a darkened house,
Where, ere his footsteps reached ripe manhood's
    brink,
Terror and anguish were his lot to drink;
I cannot rid the thought nor hold it close
But dimly dream upon that man alone:
Now though the autumn clouds most softly pass,
The cricket chides beneath the doorstep stone
And greener than the season grows the grass.
Nor can I drop my lids nor shade my brows,
But there he stands beside the lifted sash;
And with a swooning of the heart, I think
Where the black shingles slope to meet the boughs
And, shattered on the roof like smallest snows,
The tiny petals of the mountain ash.

CHRISTOPHER MARLOWE

from *Hero and Leander*, Sestiad II

By this, sad Hero, with love unacquainted,
Viewing Leander's face, fell down and fainted.
He kissed her, and breathed life into her lips,
Wherewith, as one displeased, away she trips.
Yet as she went, full often looked behind,
And many poor excuses did she find
To linger by the way, and once she stayed,
And would have turned again, but was afraid,
In offering parley, to be counted light.
So on she goes, and in her idle flight,
Her painted fan of curlèd plumes let fall,
Thinking to train Leander therewithal.
He being a novice, knew not what she meant,
But stayed, and after her a letter sent,
Which joyful Hero answered in such sort,
As he had hope to scale the beauteous fort
Wherein the liberal Graces locked their wealth,
And therefore to her tower he got by stealth.
Wide open stood the door, he need not climb,
And she herself before the pointed time
Had spread the board, with roses strewed the room,
And oft looked out, and mused he did not come.
At last he came; O who can tell the greeting
These greedy lovers had at their first meeting?
He asked, she gave, and nothing was denied;
Both to each other quickly were affied.
Look how their hands, so were their hearts united,
And what he did she willingly requited.
(Sweet are the kisses, the embracements sweet,
When like desires and affections meet,
For from the earth to heaven is Cupid raised,
Where fancy is in equal balance peised.)

Yet she this rashness suddenly repented,
And turned aside, and to herself lamented,
As if her name and honour had been wronged
By being possessed of him for whom she longed;
Ay, and she wished, albeit not from her heart,
That he would leave her turret and depart.
The mirthful god of amorous pleasure smiled
To see how he this captive nymph beguiled;
For hitherto he did but fan the fire,
And kept it down that it might mount the higher.
Now waxed she jealous, lest his love abated,
Fearing her own thoughts made her to be hated.
Therefore unto him hastily she goes,
And, like light Salmacis, her body throws
Upon his bosom, where with yielding eyes
She offers up herself a sacrifice,
To slake his anger, if he were displeased.
O what god would not therewith be appeased?
Like Aesop's cock, this jewel he enjoyèd,
And as a brother with his sister toyèd,
Supposing nothing else was to be done,
Now he her favour and good will had won.
But know you not that creatures wanting sense
By nature have a mutual appetence,
And wanting organs to advance a step,
Moved by love's force, unto each other leap?
Much more in subjects having intellect
Some hidden influence breeds like effect.
Albeit Leander, rude in love, and raw,
Long dallying with Hero, nothing saw
That might delight him more, yet he suspected
Some amorous rites or other were neglected.
Therefore unto his body hers he clung;
She, fearing on the rushes to be flung,
Strived with redoubled strength; the more she strivèd,
The more a gentle pleasing heat revivèd,
Which taught him all that elder lovers know.
And now the same 'gan so to scorch and glow,

As in plain terms (yet cunningly) he craved it;
Love always makes those eloquent that have it.
She, with a kind of granting, put him by it,
And ever as he thought himself most nigh it,
Like to the tree of Tantalus she fled,
And, seeming lavish, saved her maidenhead.
Ne'er king more sought to keep his diadem,
Than Hero this inestimable gem.
Above our life we love a steadfast friend,
Yet when a token of great worth we send,
We often kiss it, often look thereon,
And stay the messenger that would be gone:
No marvel, then, though Hero would not yield
So soon to part from that she dearly held.
Jewels being lost are found again, this never;
'Tis lost but once, and once lost, lost for ever.

ANDREW MARVELL

To His Coy Mistress

Had we but world enough, and time,
This coyness, Lady, were no crime.
We would sit down, and think which way
To walk, and pass our long love's day.
Thou by the Indian Ganges' side
Shouldst rubies find: I by the tide
Of Humber would complain. I would
Love you ten years before the flood:
And you should, if you please, refuse
Till the conversion of the Jews.
My vegetable love should grow
Vaster than empires, and more slow.
An hundred years should go to praise
Thine eyes, and on thy forehead gaze.
Two hundred to adore each breast:
But thirty thousand to the rest.
An age at least to every part,
And the last age should show your heart:
For, Lady, you deserve this state;
Nor would I love at lower rate.
    But at my back I always hear
Time's wingèd chariot hurrying near:
And yonder all before us lie
Deserts of vast eternity.
Thy beauty shall no more be found;
Nor, in thy marble vault, shall sound
My echoing song: then worms shall try
That long-preserved virginity:
And your quaint honour turn to dust;
And into ashes all my lust.
The grave's a fine and private place,
But none, I think, do there embrace.

Now, therefore, while the youthful glue
Sits on thy skin like morning dew,
And while thy willing soul transpires
At every pore with instant fires,
Now let us sport us while we may;
And now, like amorous birds of prey,
Rather at once our time devour,
Than languish in his slow-chapped power.
Let us roll all our strength, and all
Our sweetness, up into one ball:
And tear our pleasures with rough strife,
Thorough the iron grates of life.
Thus, though we cannot make our sun
Stand still, yet we will make him run.

JOHN KEATS

from *The Eve of St Agnes*

VI

They told her how, upon St Agnes' Eve,
Young virgins might have visions of delight,
And soft adorings from their loves receive
Upon the honey'd middle of the night,
If ceremonies due they did aright;
As, supperless to bed they must retire,
And couch supine their beauties, lily white;
Nor look behind, nor sideways, but require
Of Heaven with upward eyes for all that they desire.

VII

Full of this whim was thoughtful Madeline:
The music, yearning like a God in pain,
She scarcely heard: her maiden eyes divine,
Fix'd on the floor, saw many a sweeping train
Pass by – she heeded not at all: in vain
Came many a tiptoe, amorous cavalier,
And back retir'd; not cool'd by high disdain,
But she saw not: her heart was otherwhere:
She sigh'd for Agnes' dreams, the sweetest of the year.

VIII

She danc'd along with vague, regardless eyes,
Anxious her lips, her breathing quick and short:
The hallow'd hour was near at hand: she sighs
Amid the timbrels, and the throng'd resort
Of whisperers in anger, or in sport;
'Mid looks of love, defiance, hate, and scorn,
Hoodwink'd with faery fancy; all amort,
Save to St Agnes and her lambs unshorn,
And all the bliss to be before tomorrow morn.

IX

So, purposing each moment to retire,
  She linger'd still. Meantime, across the moors,
Had come young Porphyro, with heart on fire
  For Madeline. Beside the portal doors,
Buttress'd from moonlight, stands he, and implores
  All saints to give him sight of Madeline,
But for one moment in the tedious hours,
  That he might gaze and worship all unseen;
Perchance speak, kneel, touch, kiss – in sooth such
    things have been.

*   *   *

XXII

Her falt'ring hand upon the balustrade,
  Old Angela was feeling for the stair,
When Madeline, St Agnes' charmed maid,
  Rose, like a mission'd spirit, unaware:
With silver taper's light, and pious care,
  She turn'd, and down the aged gossip led
To a safe level matting. Now prepare,
  Young Porphyro, for gazing on that bed;
She comes, she comes again, like ring-dove fray'd
    and fled.

XXIII

Out went the taper as she hurried in;
  Its little smoke, in pallid moonshine, died:
She clos'd the door, she panted, all akin
  To spirits of the air, and visions wide:
No uttered syllable, or, woe betide!
  But to her heart, her heart was voluble,
Paining with eloquence her balmy side;
  As though a tongueless nightingale should swell
Her throat in vain, and die, heart-stifled, in her dell.

XXIV

A casement high and triple-arch'd there was,
All garlanded with carven imag'ries
Of fruits, and flowers, and bunches of knot-grass,
And diamonded with panes of quaint device,
Innumerable of stains and splendid dyes,
As are the tiger-moth's deep-damask'd wings;
And in the midst, 'mong thousand heraldries,
And twilight saints, and dim emblazonings,
A shielded scutcheon blush'd with blood of queens
    and kings.

XXV

Full on this casement shone the wintry moon,
And threw warm gules on Madeline's fair breast,
As down she knelt for heaven's grace and boon;
Rose-bloom fell on her hands, together prest,
And on her silver cross soft amethyst,
And on her hair a glory, like a saint:
She seem'd a splendid angel, newly drest,
Save wings, for heaven – Porphyro grew faint:
She knelt, so pure a thing, so free from mortal taint.

XXVI

Anon his heart revives: her vespers done,
Of all its wreathed pearls her hair she frees;
Unclasps her warmed jewels one by one;
Loosens her fragrant boddice; by degrees
Her rich attire creeps rustling to her knees:
Half-hidden, like a mermaid in sea-weed,
Pensive awhile she dreams awake, and sees,
In fancy, fair St Agnes in her bed,
But dares not look behind, or all the charm is fled.

XXVII

Soon, trembling in her soft and chilly nest,
In sort of wakeful swoon, perplex'd she lay,
Until the poppied warmth of sleep oppress'd
Her soothed limbs, and soul fatigued away;

Flown, like a thought, until the morrow-day;
Blissfully haven'd both from joy and pain;
Clasp'd like a missal where swart Paynims pray;
Blinded alike from sunshine and from rain,
As though a rose should shut, and be a bud again.

XXVIII

Stol'n to this paradise, and so entranced,
Porphyro gazed upon her empty dress,
And listen'd to her breathing, if it chanced
To wake into a slumberous tenderness;
Which when he heard, that minute did he bless,
And breath'd himself: then from the closet crept,
Noiseless as fear in a wide wilderness,
And over the hush'd carpet, silent, stept,
And 'tween the curtains peep'd, where, lo! – how fast she
    slept.

XXIX

Then by the bed-side, where the faded moon
Made a dim, silver twilight, soft he set
A table, and, half anguish'd, threw thereon
A cloth of woven crimson, gold, and jet –
O for some drowsy Morphean amulet!
The boisterous, midnight, festive clarion,
The kettle-drum, and far-heard clarionet,
Affray his ears, though but in dying tone –
The hall door shuts again, and all the noise is gone.

XXX

And still she slept an azure-lidded sleep,
In blanched linen, smooth, and lavender'd,
While he from forth the closet brought a heap
Of candied apple, quince, and plum, and gourd;
With jellies soother than the creamy curd,
And lucent syrops, tinct with cinnamon;
Manna and dates, in argosy transferr'd
From Fez; and spiced dainties, every one,
From silken Samarcand to cedar'd Lebanon.

XXXI

These delicates he heap'd with glowing hand
On golden dishes and in baskets bright
Of wreathed silver: sumptuous they stand
In the retired quiet of the night,
Filling the chilly room with perfume light –
'And now, my love, my seraph fair, awake!
Thou art my heaven, and I thine eremite:
Open thine eyes, for meek St Agnes' sake,
Or I shall drowse beside thee, so my soul doth ache.'

XXXII

Thus whispering, his warm, unnerved arm
Sank in her pillow. Shaded was her dream
By the dusk curtains – 'twas a midnight charm
Impossible to melt as iced stream:
The lustrous salvers in the moonlight gleam;
Broad golden fringe upon the carpet lies:
It seem'd he never, never could redeem
From such a stedfast spell his lady's eyes;
So mus'd awhile, entoil'd in woofed phantasies.

XXXIII

Awakening up, he took her hollow lute –
Tumultuous – and, in chords that tenderest be,
He play'd an ancient ditty, long since mute,
In Provence call'd, 'La belle dame sans mercy',
Close to her ear touching the melody –
Wherewith disturb'd, she utter'd a soft moan:
He ceased – she panted quick – and suddenly
Her blue affrayed eyes wide open shone:
Upon his knees he sank, pale as smooth-sculptured
stone.

XXXIV

Her eyes were open, but she still beheld,
Now wide awake, the vision of her sleep:
There was a painful change, that nigh expell'd
The blisses of her dream so pure and deep

At which fair Madeline began to weep,
And moan forth witless words with many a sigh;
While still her gaze on Porphyro would keep;
Who knelt, with joined hands and piteous eye,
Fearing to move or speak, she look'd so dreamingly.

XXXV

'Ah, Porphyro!' said she, 'but even now
Thy voice was at sweet tremble in mine ear,
Made tuneable with every sweetest vow;
And those sad eyes were spiritual and clear:
How chang'd thou art! how pallid, chill, and drear!
Give me that voice again, my Porphyro,
Those looks immortal, those complainings dear!
Oh leave me not in this eternal woe,
For if thou diest, my Love, I know not where to go.'

XXXVI

Beyond a mortal man impassion'd far
At these voluptuous accents, he arose,
Ethereal, flush'd, and like a throbbing star
Seen mid the sapphire heaven's deep repose;
Into her dream he melted, as the rose
Blendeth its odour with the violet –
Solution sweet: meantime the frost-wind blows
Like Love's alarum pattering the sharp sleet
Against the window-panes; St Agnes' moon hath set.

D. H. LAWRENCE

Green

The dawn was apple-green,
   The sky was green wine held up in the sun,
The moon was a golden petal between.

She opened her eyes, and green
   They shone, clear like flowers undone
For the first time, now for the first time seen.

E. E. CUMMINGS

i like my body when it is with your
body. It is so quite new a thing.
Muscles better and nerves more.
i like your body. i like what it does,
i like its hows. i like to feel the spine
of your body and its bones, and the trembling
-firm-smooth ness and which i will
again and again and again
kiss, i like kissing this and that of you,
i like, slowly stroking the, shocking fuzz
of your electric fur, and what-is-it comes
over parting flesh . . . And eyes big love-crumbs,

and possibly i like the thrill

of under me you so quite new

CHRISTINA G. ROSSETTI

A Birthday

My heart is like a singing bird
   Whose nest is in a watered shoot;
My heart is like an apple tree
   Whose boughs are bent with thickset fruit;
My heart is like a rainbow shell
   That paddles in a halcyon sea;
My heart is gladder than all these
   Because my love is come to me.

Raise me a dais of silk and down;
   Hang it with vair and purple dyes;
Carve it in doves and pomegranates,
   And peacocks with a hundred eyes;
Work it in gold and silver grapes,
   In leaves and silver fleurs-de-lys;
Because the birthday of my life
   Is come, my love is come to me.

WALT WHITMAN

We Two Boys together Clinging

We two boys together clinging,
One the other never leaving,
Up and down the roads going, North and South
    excursions making,
Power enjoying, elbows stretching, fingers clutching,
Arm'd and fearless, eating, drinking, sleeping, loving,
No law less than ourselves owning, sailing, soldiering,
    thieving, threatening,
Misers, menials, priests alarming, air breathing, water
    drinking, on the turf or the sea-beach dancing,
Cities wrenching, ease scorning, statutes mocking,
    feebleness chasing,
Fulfilling our foray.

A. E. HOUSMAN

from *A Shropshire Lad*: II

Loveliest of trees, the cherry now
Is hung with bloom along the bough,
And stands about the woodland ride
Wearing white for Eastertide.

Now, of my threescore years and ten,
Twenty will not come again,
And take from seventy springs a score,
It only leaves me fifty more.

And since to look at things in bloom
Fifty springs are little room,
About the woodlands I will go
To see the cherry hung with snow.

LOUIS MACNEICE

Apple Blossom

The first blossom was the best blossom
For the child who never had seen an orchard;
For the youth whom whisky had led astray
The morning after was the first day.

The first apple was the best apple
For Adam before he heard the sentence;
When the flaming sword endorsed the Fall
The trees were his to plant for all.

The first ocean was the best ocean
For the child from streets of doubt and litter;
For the youth for whom the skies unfurled
His first love was his first world.

But the first verdict seemed the worst verdict
When Adam and Eve were expelled from Eden;
Yet when the bitter gates clanged to
The sky beyond was just as blue.

For the next ocean is the first ocean
And the last ocean is the first ocean
And, however often the sun may rise,
A new thing dawns upon our eyes.

For the last blossom is the first blossom
And the first blossom is the best blossom
And when from Eden we take our way
The morning after is the first day.

Making a
Living and
Making Love

SIR HENRY WOTTON

The Character of a Happy Life

How happy is he born and taught,
That serveth not another's will;
Whose Armour is his honest thought,
And simple truth his utmost skill;

Whose passions not his Masters are;
Whose Soul is still prepar'd for Death,
Unti'd unto the World by care
Of public Fame, or private Breath;

Who envies none that chance doth raise,
Or vice; who never understood
How deepest Wounds are given by praise;
Nor Rules of State, but Rules of good;

Who hath his Life from Rumours freed;
Whose Conscience is his strong retreat;
Whose State can neither Flatterers feed,
Nor Ruin make Oppressors great;

Who God doth late and early pray
More of his Grace than Gifts to lend;
And entertains the harmless day
With a Religious book or friend!

This man is freed from servile bands
Of hope to rise, or fear to fall:
Lord of himself, though not of lands;
And having nothing, yet hath all.

BEN JONSON

from *The Alchemist*, II, i

SIR EPICURE MAMMON:

            Come on, sir. Now you set your foot on shore
In *Novo Orbe*; here's the rich Peru,
And there within, sir, are the golden mines,
Great Solomon's Ophir! He was sailing to 't
Three years, but we have reached it in ten months.
This is the day wherein, to all my friends,
I will pronounce the happy word, 'Be rich!'
This day you shall be *spectatissimi*.
You shall no more deal with the hollow die,
Or the frail card. No more be at charge of keeping
The livery-punk for the young heir, that must
Seal, at all hours, in his shirt; no more,
If he deny, ha' him beaten to 't, as he is
That brings him the commodity; no more
Shall thirst of satin, or the covetous hunger
Of velvet entrails for a rude-spun cloak,
To be displayed at Madam Augusta's, make
The sons of sword and hazard fall before
The golden calf, and on their knees, whole nights,
Commit idolatry with wine and trumpets,
Or go a-feasting after drum and ensign.
No more of this. You shall start up young viceroys,
And have your punks and punketees, my Surly.
And unto thee I speak it first, 'Be rich!'

JOHN DAVIDSON
Thirty Bob a Week

I couldn't touch a stop and turn a screw,
  And set the blooming world a-work for me,
Like such as cut their teeth – I hope, like you –
  On the handle of a skeleton gold key;
I cut mine on a leek, which I eat it every week:
  I'm a clerk at thirty bob as you can see.

But I don't allow it's luck and all a toss;
  There's no such thing as being starred and
      crossed;
It's just the power of some to be a boss,
  And the bally power of others to be bossed:
I face the music, sir; you bet I ain't a cur;
  Strike me lucky if I don't believe I'm lost!

For like a mole I journey in the dark,
  A-travelling along the underground
From my Pillar'd Halls and broad Suburbean Park,
  To come the daily dull official round;
And home again at night with my pipe all alight,
  A-scheming how to count ten bob a pound.

And it's often very cold and very wet,
  And my missis stitches towels for a hunks;
And the Pillar'd Halls is half of it to let –
  Three rooms about the size of travelling trunks,
And we cough, my wife and I, to dislocate a sigh,
  When the noisy little kids are in their bunks.

But you never hear her do a growl or whine,
    For she's made of flint and roses, very odd;
And I've got to cut my meaning rather fine,
    Or I'd blubber, for I'm made of greens and sod:
So p'r'aps we are in Hell for all that I can tell,
    And lost and damn'd and served up hot to God.

I ain't blaspheming, Mr Silver-tongue;
    I'm saying things a bit beyond your art:
Of all the rummy starts you ever sprung,
    Thirty bob a week's the rummiest start!
With your science and your books and your the'ries
        about spooks,
    Did you ever hear of looking in your heart?

I didn't mean your pocket, Mr, no:
    I mean that having children and a wife,
With thirty bob on which to come and go,
    Isn't dancing to the tabor and the fife:
When it doesn't make you drink, by Heaven! it
        makes you think,
    And notice curious items about life.

I step into my heart and there I meet
    A god-almighty devil singing small,
Who would like to shout and whistle in the street,
    And squelch the passers flat against the wall;
If the whole world was a cake he had the power to take,
    He would take it, ask for more, and eat them all.

And I meet a sort of simpleton beside,
    The kind that life is always giving beans;
With thirty bob a week to keep a bride
    He fell in love and married in his teens:
At thirty bob he stuck; but he knows it isn't luck:
    He knows the seas are deeper than tureens.

And the god-almighty devil and the fool
    That meet me in the High Street on the strike,
When I walk about my heart a-gathering wool,
    Are my good and evil angels if you like.
And both of them together in every kind of weather
    Ride me like a double-seated bike.

That's rough a bit and needs its meaning curled.
    But I have a high old hot un in my mind –
A most engrugious notion of the world,
    That leaves your lightning 'rithmetic behind:
I give it at a glance when I say 'There ain't no
        chance,
    Nor nothing of the lucky-lottery kind.'

And it's this way that I make it out to be:
    No fathers, mothers, countries, climates – none;
Not Adam was responsible for me,
    Nor society, nor systems, nary one:
A little sleeping seed, I woke – I did, indeed –
    A million years before the blooming sun.

I woke because I thought the time had come;
    Beyond my will there was no other cause;
And everywhere I found myself at home,
    Because I chose to be the thing I was;
And in whatever shape of mollusc or of ape
    I always went according to the laws.

I was the love that chose my mother out;
    I joined two lives and from the union burst;
My weakness and my strength without a doubt
    Are mine alone forever from the first:
It's just the very same with a difference in the name
    As 'Thy will be done.' You say it if you durst!

They say it daily up and down the land
    As easy as you take a drink, it's true;
But the difficultest go to understand,
    And the difficultest job a man can do,
Is to come it brave and meek with thirty bob a week,
    And feel that that's the proper thing for you.

It's a naked child against a hungry wolf;
    It's playing bowls upon a splitting wreck;
It's walking on a string across a gulf
    With millstones fore-and-aft about your neck;
But the thing is daily done by many and many a one;
    And we fall, face forward, fighting, on the deck.

THEODORE ROETHKE

Dolor

I have known the inexorable sadness of pencils,
Neat in their boxes, dolor of pad and paper-weight,
All the misery of manilla folders and mucilage,
Desolation in immaculate public places,
Lonely reception room, lavatory, switchboard,
The unalterable pathos of basin and pitcher,
Ritual of multigraph, paper-clip, comma,
Endless duplication of lives and objects.
And I have seen dust from the walls of institutions,
Finer than flour, alive, more dangerous than silica,
Sift, almost invisible, through long afternoons of tedium,
Dropping a fine film on nails and delicate eyebrows,
Glazing the pale hair, the duplicate grey standard faces.

THOMAS HOOD

The Song of the Shirt

With fingers weary and worn,
   With eyelids heavy and red,
A Woman sat, in unwomanly rags,
   Plying her needle and thread –
     Stitch! stitch! stitch!
In poverty, hunger, and dirt,
   And still with a voice of dolorous pitch
She sang the 'Song of the Shirt'!

  'Work! work! work!
While the cock is crowing aloof!
   And work – work – work,
Till the stars shine through the roof!
It's O! to be a slave
   Along with the barbarous Turk,
Where woman has never a soul to save,
   If this is Christian work!

  Work – work – work
Till the brain begins to swim;
   Work – work – work
Till the eyes are heavy and dim!
Seam, and gusset, and band,
   Band, and gusset, and seam,
     Till over the buttons I fall asleep,
   And sew them on in a dream!

O! Men, with Sisters dear!
   O! Men! with Mothers and Wives!
It is not linen you're wearing out,
   But human creatures' lives!

Stitch – stitch – stitch,
   In poverty, hunger and dirt,
Sewing at once, with a double thread,
   A Shroud as well as a Shirt.

But why do I talk of Death?
   That Phantom of grisly bone,
I hardly fear its terrible shape,
   It seems so like my own –
   It seems so like my own,
   Because of the fasts I keep,
Oh! God! that bread should be so dear,
   And flesh and blood so cheap!

   Work – work – work!
      My labour never flags;
And what are its wages? A bed of straw,
   A crust of bread – and rags.
That shatter'd roof – and this naked floor –
   A table – a broken chair –
And a wall so blank, my shadow I thank
   For sometimes falling there!

   Work – work – work!
From weary chime to chime,
   Work – work – work –
As prisoners work for crime!
   Band, and gusset, and seam,
   Seam, and gusset, and band,
Till the heart is sick, and the brain benumb'd,
   As well as the weary hand.

   Work – work – work,
In the dull December light,
   And work – work – work,
When the weather is warm and bright!

While underneath the eaves
  The brooding swallows cling
As if to show me their sunny backs
  And twit me with the spring.

  Oh! but to breathe the breath
Of the cowslip and primrose sweet –
  With the sky above my head,
And the grass beneath my feet,
For only one short hour
  To feel as I used to feel,
Before I knew the woes of want
  And the walk that costs a meal!

Oh! but for one short hour!
    A respite however brief!
No blessed leisure for Love or Hope,
    But only time for Grief!
A little weeping would ease my heart,
    But in their briny bed
My tears must stop, for every drop
    Hinders needle and thread!'

With fingers weary and worn,
  With eyelids heavy and red,
A Woman sate in unwomanly rags,
  Plying her needle and thread –
    Stitch! stitch! stitch!
  In poverty, hunger, and dirt,
And still with a voice of dolorous pitch,
Would that its tone could reach the Rich!
  She sang this 'Song of the Shirt'!

LINTON KWESI JOHNSON

More Time

wi mawchin out di ole towards di new centri
arm wid di new teknalagy
wi gettin more an more producktivity
some seh tings lookin-up fi prasperity
but if evrywan goin get a share dis time
ole mentality mus get lef behine

wi want di shatah workin day
gi wi di shatah workin week
langah holiday
wi need decent pay

more time fi leasure
more time fi pleasure
more time fi edificaeshun
more time fi reckreashan
more time fi contemplate
more time fi ruminate
more time fi relate
more time
wi need
more
time
gi wi more time

a full time dem abalish unemployment
an revalueshanize laybah deployment
a full time dem banish owevahtime
mek evrybady get a wok dis time

wi need a highah quality a livity
wi need it now an fi evrybady

wi need di shatah workin year
gi wi di shatah workin life
more time fi di huzban
more time fi di wife
more time fi di children
more time fi wi fren dem
more time fi meditate
more time fi create
more time fi livin
more time fi life
more time
wi need more time
gi wi more time

PHILIP LARKIN

Toads

Why should I let the toad *work*
    Squat on my life?
Can't I use my wit as a pitchfork
    And drive the brute off?

Six days of the week it soils
    With its sickening poison –
Just for paying a few bills!
    That's out of proportion.

Lots of folk live on their wits:
    Lecturers, lispers,
Losels, loblolly-men, louts –
    They don't end as paupers;

Lots of folk live up lanes
    With fires in a bucket,
Eat windfalls and tinned sardines –
    They seem to like it.

Their nippers have got bare feet,
    Their unspeakable wives
Are skinny as whippets – and yet
    No one actually *starves*.

Ah, were I courageous enough
    To shout *Stuff your pension!*
But I know, all too well, that's the stuff
    That dreams are made on:

For something sufficiently toad-like
    Squats in me, too;
Its hunkers are heavy as hard luck,
    And cold as snow,

And will never allow me to blarney
    My way to getting
The fame and the girl and the money
    All at one sitting.

I don't say, one bodies the other
    One's spiritual truth;
But I do say it's hard to lose either,
    When you have both.

WILLIAM WORDSWORTH

The world is too much with us; late and soon,
Getting and spending, we lay waste our powers:
Little we see in nature that is ours;
We have given our hearts away, a sordid boon!
This Sea that bares her bosom to the moon;
The Winds that will be howling at all hours
And are up-gathered now like sleeping flowers;
For this, for every thing, we are out of tune;
It moves us not – Great God! I'd rather be
A Pagan suckled in a creed outworn;
So might I, standing on this pleasant lea,
Have glimpses that would make me less forlorn;
Have sight of Proteus coming from the sea;
Or hear old Triton blow his wreathed horn.

CAROL ANN DUFFY

Mrs Sisyphus

That's him pushing the stone up the hill, the jerk.
I call it a stone – it's nearer the size of a kirk.
When he first started out, it just used to irk,
but now it incenses me, and him, the absolute berk.
I could do something vicious to him with a dirk.

Think of the perks, he says.
What use is a perk, I shriek,
when you haven't the time to pop open a cork
or go for so much as a walk in the park?
He's a dork.
Folk flock from miles around just to gawk.
They think it's a quirk,
a bit of a lark.
A load of old bollocks is nearer the mark.
He might as well bark
at the moon –
that feckin' stone's no sooner up
than it's rolling back
all the way down.
And what does he say?
Mustn't shirk –
keen as a hawk,
lean as a shark
Mustn't shirk!

DEREK WALCOTT

Ebb

Year round, year round, we'll ride
this treadmill whose frayed tide
fretted with mud

leaves our suburban shoreline littered
with rainbow muck, the afterbirth
of industry, past scurf-

streaked bungalows
and pioneer factory;
but, blessedly, it narrows

through a dark aisle
of fountaining, gold coconuts, an oasis
marked for the yellow Caterpillar tractor.

We'll watch this shovelled too, but as we file
through its swift-wickered shade there always is
some island schooner netted in its weave

like a lamed heron
an oil-crippled gull;
a few more yards upshore

and it heaves free,
it races the horizon
with us, railed to one law,

ruled, like the washed-up moon
to circle her lost zone,
her radiance thinned.

The palm fronds signal wildly in the wind,
but we are bound elsewhere,
from the last sacred wood.

The schooner's out too far,
too far that boyhood.
Sometimes I turn to see

the schooner, crippled, try to tread the air,
the moon break in sere sail,
but without envy.

For safety, each sunfall,
the wildest of us all
mortgages life to fear.

And why not? From this car
there's terror enough in the habitual,
miracle enough in the familiar. Sure . . .

ARTHUR CLOUGH

Say Not the Struggle Nought Availeth

Say not the struggle nought availeth,
   The labour and the wounds are vain,
The enemy faints not, nor faileth,
   And as things have been they remain.

If hopes were dupes, fears may be liars;
   It may be, in yon smoke concealed,
Your comrades chase e'en now the fliers,
   And, but for you, possess the field.

For while the tired waves, vainly breaking,
   Seem here no painful inch to gain,
Far back, through creeks and inlets making,
   Comes silent, flooding in, the main,

And not by eastern windows only,
   When daylight comes, comes in the light,
In front, the sun climbs slow, how slowly,
   But westward, look, the land is bright.

SAMUEL TAYLOR COLERIDGE

Work Without Hope

All Nature seems at work. Slugs leave their lair –
The bees are stirring – birds are on the wing –
And Winter slumbering in the open air,
Wears on his smiling face a dream of Spring!
And I, the while, the sole unbusy thing,
Nor honey make, nor pair, nor build, nor sing.

Yet well I ken the banks where amaranths blow,
Have traced the fount whence streams of nectar flow.
Bloom, O ye amaranths! bloom for whom ye may,
For me ye bloom not! Glide, rich streams, away!
With lips unbrightened, wreathless brow, I stroll:
And would you learn the spells that drowse my soul?
Work without hope draws nectar in a sieve,
And hope without an object cannot live.

JOHN MILTON

from *Paradise Lost*, Book IV

Now came still ev'ning on, and twilight grey
Had in her sober livery all things clad;
Silence accompanied, for beast and bird,
They to their grassy couch, these to their nests
Were slunk, all but the wakeful nightingale;
She all night long her amorous descant sung;
Silence was pleased: now glowed the firmament
With living sapphires: Hesperus that led
The starry host, rode brightest, till the moon
Rising in clouded majesty, at length
Apparent queen unveiled her peerless light,
And o'er the dark her silver mantle threw.
    When Adam thus to Eve: Fair consort, th' hour
Of night, and all things now retired to rest
Mind us of like repose, since God hath set
Labour and rest, as day and night to men
Successive, and the timely dew of sleep
Now falling with soft slumb'rous weight inclines
Our eye-lids; other creatures all day long
Rove idle unemployed, and less need rest;
Man hath his daily work of body or mind
Appointed, which declares his dignity,
And the regard of Heav'n on all his ways;
While other animals unactive range,
And of their doings God takes no account.
Tomorrow ere fresh morning streak the east
With first approach of light, we must be ris'n,
And at our pleasant labour, to reform
Yon flow'ry arbours, yonder alleys green,
Our walk at noon, with branches overgrown,
That mock our scant manuring, and require
More hands than ours to lop their wanton growth:

Those blossoms also, and those dropping gums,
That lie bestrewn unsightly and unsmooth,
Ask riddance, if we mean to tread with ease;
Meanwhile, as nature wills, night bids us rest.

W. H. DAVIES

Leisure

What is this life if, full of care,
We have no time to stand and stare.

No time to stand beneath the boughs
And stare as long as sheep or cows.

No time to see, when woods we pass,
Where squirrels hide their nuts in grass.

No time to see, in broad daylight,
Streams full of stars like skies at night.

No time to turn at Beauty's glance,
And watch her feet, how they can dance.

No time to wait till her mouth can
Enrich that smile her eyes began.

A poor life this if, full of care,
We have no time to stand and stare.

LOUIS MACNEICE

Meeting Point

Time was away and somewhere else,
There were two glasses and two chairs
And two people with the one pulse
(Somebody stopped the moving stairs):
Time was away and somewhere else.

And they were neither up nor down;
The stream's music did not stop
Flowing through heather, limpid brown,
Although they sat in a coffee shop
And they were neither up nor down.

The bell was silent in the air
Holding its inverted poise –
Between the clang and clang a flower,
A brazen calyx of no noise:
The bell was silent in the air.

The camels crossed the miles of sand
That stretched around the cups and plates;
The desert was their own, they planned
To portion out the stars and dates:
The camels crossed the miles of sand.

Time was away and somewhere else.
The waiter did not come, the clock
Forgot them and the radio waltz
Came out like water from a rock:
Time was away and somewhere else.

Her fingers flicked away the ash
That bloomed again in tropic trees:
Not caring if the markets crash
When they had forests such as these,
Her fingers flicked away the ash.

God or whatever means the Good
Be praised that time can stop like this,
That what the heart has understood
Can verify in the body's peace
God or whatever means the Good.

Time was away and she was here
And life no longer what it was,
The bell was silent in the air
And all the room one glow because
Time was away and she was here.

RICHARD BARNFIELD

Sighing, and sadly sitting by my Love,
He ask'd the cause of my heart's sorrowing,
Conjuring me by heaven's eternal King
To tell the cause which me so much did move.
Compell'd: (quoth I) to thee will I confess,
Love is the cause; and only love it is
That doth deprive me of my heavenly bliss.
Love is the pain that doth my heart oppress.
And what is she (quoth he) whom thou dos't love?
Look in this glass (quoth I) there shalt thou see
The perfect form of my felicity.
When, thinking that it would strange Magic prove,
He open'd it: and taking off the cover,
He straight perceiv'd himself to be my Lover.

BEN OKRI

I Held You in the Square

I held you in the square
And felt the evening
Re-order itself around
Your smile.

The dreams I could never touch
Felt like your body.
Your gentleness made the
Night soft.

And even if we didn't know
Where we were going,
Nor what street to take
Or what bench to sit on
What chambers awaited
That would deliver us our
Naked joy,
I could feel in your spirit
The restlessness for a journey
Whose beauty lies
In the arriving moment
Of each desire.

Holding you in the evening square,
I sealed a dream
With your smile as the secret pact.

March 1986

THOMAS MOORE

Did Not

'Twas a new feeling – something more
Than we had dared to own before,
    Which then we hid not;
We saw it in each other's eye,
And wish'd, in every half-breath'd sigh,
    To speak, but did not.

She felt my lips' impassioned touch –
'Twas the first time I dared so much,
    And yet she chid not;
But whisper'd o'er my burning brow,
'Oh! do you doubt I love you now?'
    Sweet soul! I did not.

Warmly I felt her bosom thrill,
I press'd it closer, closer still,
    Though gently bid not;
Till – oh! the world hath seldom heard
Of lovers, who so nearly err'd,
    And yet, who did not.

FLEUR ADCOCK

Against Coupling

I write in praise of the solitary act:
of not feeling a trespassing tongue
forced into one's mouth, one's breath
smothered, nipples crushed against the
ribcage, and that metallic tingling
in the chin set off by a certain odd nerve:

unpleasure. Just to avoid those eyes would help –
such eyes as a young girl draws life from,
listening to the vegetal
rustle within her, as his gaze
stirs polypal fronds in the obscure
sea-bed of her body, and her own eyes blur.

There is much to be said for abandoning
this no longer novel exercise –
for not 'participating in
a total experience' – when
one feels like the lady in Leeds who
had seen *The Sound of Music* eighty-six times;

or more, perhaps, like the school drama mistress
producing *A Midsummer Night's Dream*
for the seventh year running, with
yet another cast from 5B.
Pyramus and Thisbe are dead, but
the hole in the wall can still be troublesome.

I advise you, then, to embrace it without
encumbrance. No need to set the scene,
dress up (or undress), make speeches.
Five minutes of solitude are
enough – in the bath, or to fill
that gap between the Sunday papers and lunch.

OGDEN NASH

Reflections on Ice-Breaking

Candy
Is dandy
But liquor
Is quicker.

EDMUND WALLER

To Phillis

Phillis, why should we delay
Pleasures shorter than the Day?
Can we (which we never can)
Stretch our lives beyond their Span,
Beauty, like a Shadow, flies,
And our Youth before us Dies.
Or, would Youth and Beauty stay,
Love hath Wings, and will away.
Love hath swifter Wings than Time;
Change in Love to Heaven doth climb.
Gods that never change their state
Vary oft their Love and Hate.
Phillis, to this Truth we owe
All the Love betwixt us two.
Let not you and I require
What has been our past desire;
On what Shepherds you have smil'd,
Or what Nymphs I have beguil'd;
Leave it to the Planets too,
What we shall hereafter do;
For the Joys we now may prove,
Take advice of present Love.

LADY MARY WORTLEY MONTAGU

[A Summary of Lord Lyttleton's 'Advice to a lady']

Be plain in Dress and sober in your Diet;
In short my Dearee, kiss me, and be quiet.

KIM ADDONIZIO

For Desire

Give me the strongest cheese, the one that stinks best;
and I want the good wine, the swirl in crystal
surrendering the bruised scent of blackberries,
or cherries, the rich spurt in the back
of the throat, the holding it there before swallowing.
Give me the lover who yanks open the door
of his house and presses me to the wall
in the dim hallway, and keeps me there until I'm drenched
and shaking, whose kisses arrive by the boatload
and begin their delicious diaspora
through the cities and small towns of my body.
To hell with the saints, with the martyrs
of my childhood meant to instruct me
in the power of endurance and faith,
to hell with the next world and its pallid angels
swooning and sighing like Victorian girls.
I want this world. I want to walk into
the ocean and feel it trying to drag me along
like I'm nothing but a broken bit of scratched glass,
and I want to resist it. I want to go
staggering and flailing my way
through the bars and back rooms,
through the gleaming hotels and the weedy
lots of abandoned sunflowers and the parks
where dogs are let off their leashes
in spite of the signs, where they sniff each
other and roll together in the grass, I want to
lie down somewhere and suffer for love until
it nearly kills me, and then I want to get up again
and put on that little black dress and wait
for you, yes you, to come over here
and get down on your knees and tell me
just how fucking good I look.

ROBERT HERRICK

Delight in Disorder

A sweet disorder in the dress
Kindles in clothes a wantonness;
A lawn about the shoulders thrown
Into a fine distraction;
An erring lace, which here and there
Inthralls the crimson stomacher;
A cuff neglectful, and thereby
Ribands to flow confusedly;
A winning wave, deserving note,
In the tempestuous petticoat;
A careless shoe-string, in whose tie
I see a wild civility;
Do more bewitch me, than when art
Is too precise in every part.

CHRISTOPHER MARLOWE

from *Ovid's Elegies*, Book I

Elegia V

Corinnae concubitus

In summer's heat, and mid-time of the day,
To rest my limbs upon a bed I lay;
One window shut, the other open stood,
Which gave such light as twinkles in a wood,
Like twilight glimpse at setting of the sun,
Or night being past, and yet not day begun.
Such light to shamefast maidens must be shown,
Where they may sport and seem to be unknown.
Then came Corinna in a long loose gown,
Her white neck hid with tresses hanging down,
Resembling fair Semiramis going to bed,
Or Lais of a thousand wooers sped.
I snatched her gown; being thin, the harm was small,
Yet strived she to be covered therewithal,
And striving thus as one that would be cast,
Betrayed herself, and yielded at the last.
Stark naked as she stood before mine eye,
Not one wen in her body could I spy.
What arms and shoulders did I touch and see,
How apt her breasts were to be pressed by me!
How smooth a belly under her waist saw I,
How large a leg, and what a lusty thigh!
To leave the rest, all liked me passing well;
I clinged her naked body, down she fell.
Judge you the rest: being tired she bade me kiss;
Jove send me more such afternoons as this.

CHARLES SIMIC

Crazy about Her Shrimp

We don't even take time
To come up for air.
We keep our mouths full and busy
Eating bread and cheese
And smooching in between.

No sooner have we made love
Than we are back in the kitchen.
While I chop the hot peppers,
She wiggles her ass
And stirs the shrimp on the stove.

How good the wine tastes
That has run red
Out of a laughing mouth!
Down her chin
And onto her naked tits.

'I'm getting fat,' she says,
Turning this way and that way
Before the mirror.
'I'm crazy about her shrimp!'
I shout to the gods above.

EMILY DICKINSON

Wild Nights – Wild Nights!
Were I with thee
Wild Nights should be
Our luxury!

Futile – the Winds –
To a Heart in port –
Done with the Compass –
Done with the Chart!

Rowing in Eden –
Ah, the Sea!
Might I but moor – Tonight –
In Thee!

JOHN DONNE

The Ecstasy

Where, like a pillow on a bed,
  A pregnant bank swelled up, to rest
The violet's reclining head,
  Sat we two, one another's best;

Our hands were firmly cemented
  With a fast balm, which thence did spring,
Our eye-beams twisted, and did thread
  Our eyes, upon one double string;

So to' intergraft our hands, as yet
  Was all our means to make us one,
And pictures in our eyes to get
  Was all our propagation.

As 'twixt two equal armies, Fate
  Suspends uncertain victory,
Our souls, (which to advance their state,
  Were gone out), hung 'twixt her, and me.

And whilst our souls negotiate there,
  We like sepulchral statues lay;
All day, the same our postures were,
  And we said nothing, all the day.

If any, so by love refined,
  That he soul's language understood,
And by good love were grown all mind,
  Within convenient distance stood,

He (though he knew not which soul spake
      Because both meant, both spake the same)
Might thence a new concoction take,
      And part far purer than he came.

This ecstasy doth unperplex
      (We said) and tell us what we love,
We see by this, it was not sex,
      We see, we saw not what did move:

But as all several souls contain
      Mixture of things, they know not what,
Love, these mixed souls doth mix again,
      And makes both one, each this and that.

A single violet transplant,
      The strength, the colour, and the size,
(All which before was poor, and scant,)
      Redoubles still, and multiplies.

When love, with one another so
      Interinanimates two souls,
That abler soul, which thence doth flow,
      Defects of loneliness controls.

We then, who are this new soul, know,
      Of what we are composed, and made,
For, th' atomies of which we grow,
      Are souls, whom no change can invade.

But O alas, so long, so far
      Our bodies why do we forbear?
They are ours, though they are not we, we are
      The intelligences, they the sphere.

We owe them thanks, because they thus,
      Did us, to us, at first convey,
Yielded their forces, sense, to us,
      Nor are dross to us, but allay.

On man heaven's influence works not so,
    But that it first imprints the air,
So soul into the soul may flow,
    Though it to body first repair.

As our blood labours to beget
    Spirits, as like souls as it can,
Because such fingers need to knit
    That subtle knot, which makes us man:

So must pure lovers' souls descend
    T' affections, and to faculties,
Which sense may reach and apprehend,
    Else a great prince in prison lies.

To our bodies turn we then, that so
    Weak men on love revealed may look;
Love's mysteries in souls do grow,
    But yet the body is his book.

And if some lover, such as we,
    Have heard this dialogue of one,
Let him still mark us, he shall see
    Small change, when we'are to bodies gone.

DAVID CONSTANTINE

'As our bloods separate'

As our bloods separate the clock resumes,
I hear the wind again as our hearts quieten.
We were a ring: the clock ticked round us
For that time and the wind was deflected.

The clock pecks everything to the bone.
The wind enters through the broken eyes
Of houses and through their wide mouths
And scatters the ashes from the hearth.

Sleep. Do not let go my hand.

from *The Princess*

Now sleeps the crimson petal, now the white;
Nor waves the cypress in the palace walk;
Nor winks the gold fin in the porphyry font:
The fire-fly wakens: waken thou with me.

Now droops the milkwhite peacock like a ghost,
And like a ghost she glimmers on to me.

Now lies the Earth all Danaë to the stars,
And all thy heart lies open unto me.

Now slides the silent meteor on, and leaves
A shining furrow, as thy thoughts in me.

Now folds the lily all her sweetness up,
And slips into the bosom of the lake:
So fold thyself, my dearest, thou, and slip
Into my bosom and be lost in me.

ARTHUR SYMONS
White Heliotrope

The feverish room and that white bed,
  The tumbled skirts upon a chair,
  The novel flung half-open, where
Hat, hair-pins, puffs, and paints, are spread;

The mirror that has sucked your face
  Into its secret deep of deeps;
  And there mysteriously keeps
Forgotten memories of grace;

And you, half dressed and half awake,
  Your slant eyes strangely watching me,
  And I, who watch you drowsily,
With eyes that, having slept not, ache;

This (need one dread? nay, dare one hope?)
  Will rise, a ghost of memory, if
  Ever again my handkerchief
Is scented with White Heliotrope.

ROBERT BROWNING

Two in the Campagna

I wonder do you feel today
   As I have felt since, hand in hand,
We sat down on the grass, to stray
   In spirit better through the land,
This morn of Rome and May?

For me, I touched a thought, I know,
   Has tantalized me many times,
(Like turns of thread the spiders throw
   Mocking across our path) for rhymes
To catch at and let go.

Help me to hold it! First it left
   The yellowing fennel, run to seed
There, branching from the brickwork's cleft,
   Some old tomb's ruin: yonder weed
Took up the floating weft,

Where one small orange cup amassed
   Five beetles, – blind and green they grope
Among the honey-meal: and last,
   Everywhere on the grassy slope
I traced it. Hold it fast!

The champaign with its endless fleece
   Of feathery grasses everywhere!
Silence and passion, joy and peace,
   An everlasting wash of air –
Rome's ghost since her decease.

Such life here, through such lengths of hours,
　　Such miracles performed in play,
Such primal naked forms of flowers,
　　Such letting nature have her way
While heaven looks from its towers!

How say you? Let us, O my dove,
　　Let us be unashamed of soul,
As earth lies bare to heaven above!
　　How is it under our control
To love or not to love?

I would that you were all to me,
　　You that are just so much, no more.
Nor yours nor mine, nor slave nor free!
　　Where does the fault lie? What the core
O' the wound, since wound must be?

I would I could adopt your will,
　　See with your eyes, and set my heart
Beating by yours, and drink my fill
　　At your soul's springs, – your part my part
In life, for good and ill.

No. I yearn upward, touch you close,
　　Then stand away. I kiss your cheek,
Catch your soul's warmth, – I pluck the rose
　　And love it more than tongue can speak –
Then the good minute goes.

Already how am I so far
　　Out of that minute? Must I go
Still like the thistle-ball, no bar,
　　Onward, whenever light winds blow,
Fixed by no friendly star?

Just when I seemed about to learn!
  Where is the thread now? Off again!
The old trick! Only I discern –
  Infinite passion, and the pain
Of finite hearts that yearn.

LEMN SISSAY

Love Poem

You remind me
define me
incline me.

If you died
I'd.

Family Life,
for Better,
for Worse

CHRISTOPHER MARLOWE

The Passionate Shepherd to His Love

Come live with me, and be my love,
And we will all the pleasures prove
That valleys, groves, hills and fields,
Woods, or steepy mountain yields.

And we will sit upon the rocks,
Seeing the shepherds feed their flocks
By shallow rivers, to whose falls
Melodious birds sing madrigals.

And I will make thee beds of roses,
And a thousand fragrant posies,
A cap of flowers, and a kirtle,
Embroidered all with leaves of myrtle.

A gown made of the finest wool
Which from our pretty lambs we pull,
Fair linèd slippers for the cold,
With buckles of the purest gold.

A belt of straw and ivy-buds,
With coral clasps and amber studs,
And if these pleasures may thee move,
Come live with me, and be my love.

The shepherd swains shall dance and sing
For thy delight each May morning.
If these delights thy mind may move,
Then live with me, and be my love.

EDWIN MUIR

The Confirmation

Yes, yours, my love, is the right human face.
I in my mind had waited for this long,
Seeing the false and searching for the true,
Then found you as a traveller finds a place
Of welcome suddenly amid the wrong
Valleys and rocks and twisting roads. But you,
What shall I call you? A fountain in a waste,
A well of water in a country dry,
Or anything that's honest and good, an eye
That makes the whole world bright. Your open heart,
Simple with giving, gives the primal deed,
The first good world, the blossom, the blowing seed,
The hearth, the steadfast land, the wandering sea,
Not beautiful or rare in every part,
But like yourself, as they were meant to be.

JOHN BETJEMAN

The Subaltern's Love-song

Miss J. Hunter Dunn, Miss J. Hunter Dunn,
Furnish'd and burnish'd by Aldershot sun,
What strenuous singles we played after tea,
We in the tournament – you against me!

Love-thirty, love-forty, oh! weakness of joy,
The speed of a swallow, the grace of a boy,
With carefullest carelessness, gaily you won,
I am weak from your loveliness, Joan Hunter Dunn.

Miss Joan Hunter Dunn, Miss Joan Hunter Dunn,
How mad I am, sad I am, glad that you won.
The warm-handled racket is back in its press,
But my shock-headed victor, she loves me no less.

Her father's euonymus shines as we walk,
And swing past the summer-house, buried in talk,
And cool the verandah that welcomes us in
To the six-o'clock news and a lime-juice and gin.

The scent of the conifers, sound of the bath,
The view from my bedroom of moss-dappled path,
As I struggle with double-end evening tie,
For we dance at the Golf Club, my victor and I.

On the floor of her bedroom lie blazer and shorts
And the cream-coloured walls are be-trophied with sports,
And westering, questioning settles the sun
On your low-leaded window, Miss Joan Hunter Dunn.

The Hillman is waiting, the light's in the hall,
The pictures of Egypt are bright on the wall,
My sweet, I am standing beside the oak stair
And there on the landing's the light on your hair.

By roads 'not adopted', by woodlanded ways,
She drove to the club in the late summer haze,
Into nine-o'clock Camberley, heavy with bells
And mushroomy, pine-woody, evergreen smells.

Miss Joan Hunter Dunn, Miss Joan Hunter Dunn,
I can hear from the car-park the dance has begun.
Oh! full Surrey twilight! importunate band!
Oh! strongly adorable tennis-girl's hand!

Around us are Rovers and Austins afar,
Above us, the intimate roof of the car,
And here on my right is the girl of my choice,
With the tilt of her nose and the chime of her voice,

And the scent of her wrap, and the words never said,
And the ominous, ominous dancing ahead.
We sat in the car park till twenty to one
And now I'm engaged to Miss Joan Hunter Dunn.

WILLIAM BLAKE

from *An Island in the Moon*

Hail Matrimony, made of Love!
To thy wide gates how great a drove
On purpose to be yok'd do come;
Widows and Maids and Youths also,
That lightly trip on beauty's toe,
Or sit on beauty's bum.

Hail fingerfooted lovely Creatures!
The females of our human natures,
Formed to suckle all Mankind.
'Tis you that come in time of need,
Without you we should never breed,
Or any comfort find.

For if a Damsel's blind or lame,
Or Nature's hand has crook'd her frame,
Or if she's deaf, or is wall-eyed;
Yet, if her heart is well inclin'd,
Some tender lover she shall find
That panteth for a Bride.

The universal Poultice this,
To cure whatever is amiss
In Damsel or in Widow gay!
It makes them smile, it makes them skip;
Like birds, just cured of the pip,
They chirp and hop away.

Then come, ye maidens! come, ye swains!
Come and be cur'd of all your pains
In Matrimony's Golden Cage –

EDMUND SPENSER

from *Prothalamion*

Ye gentle Birds, the world's fair ornament,
And heaven's glories, whom this happy hour
Doth lead unto your lover's blissful bower,
Joy may you have and gentle heart's content
Of your love's couplement:
And let faire *Venus*, that is Queen of love,
With her heart-quelling Sun upon you smile,
Whose smile they say, hath virtue to remove
All Love's dislike, and friendship's faulty guile
For ever to assoil.
Let endless Peace your steadfast hearts accord,
And blessed Plenty wait upon your board,
And let your bed with pleasures chaste abound,
That fruitful issue may to you afford:
Which may your foes confound,
And make your joys redound,
Upon your Bridal day, which is not long:
Sweet *Thames* run softly, till I end my Song.

EDWARD LEAR

The Owl and the Pussy-cat

The Owl and the Pussy-cat went to sea
   In a beautiful pea-green boat,
They took some honey, and plenty of money,
   Wrapped up in a five-pound note.
The Owl looked up to the stars above,
   And sang to a small guitar,
'O lovely Pussy! O Pussy, my love,
   What a beautiful Pussy you are,
        You are,
        You are!
What a beautiful Pussy you are!'

Pussy said to the Owl, 'You elegant fowl!
   How charmingly sweet you sing!
O let us be married! too long we have tarried:
   But what shall we do for a ring?'
They sailed away, for a year and a day,
   To the land where the Bong-tree grows,
And there in a wood a Piggy-wig stood,
   With a ring at the end of his nose,
        His nose,
        His nose,
With a ring at the end of his nose.

'Dear Pig, are you willing to sell for one shilling
    Your ring?' Said the Piggy, 'I will.'
So they took it away, and were married next day
    By the Turkey who lives on the hill.
They dined on mince, and slices of quince,
    Which they ate with a runcible spoon;
And hand in hand, on the edge of the sand,
    They danced by the light of the moon,
            The moon,
            The moon,
They danced by the light of the moon.

CARMEN BUGAN

A house of stone

for Mark and Ella

In the village where I was born, we wish
A house of stone to shelter the heart of the marriage

So here too, I wish you
Obstinate, strong love, unyielding and unending.

May you be in reach of each other when all seems lost,
May your tears and your smiles happen always face to
    face.

When you imagine that you have shared everything
May you know that you still have the rest of your lives
To do all of it again and again.

But now listen to the hurry of bells and
Look how petals of roses about the vineyard

Bring you the words, 'husband' and 'wife':
First words in your house of stone.

WILLIAM SHAKESPEARE

Sonnet 116

Let me not to the marriage of true minds
Admit impediments; love is not love
Which alters when it alteration finds,
Or bends with the remover to remove.
O no, it is an ever-fixèd mark
That looks on tempests and is never shaken;
It is the star to every wandering bark,
Whose worth's unknown, although his height be taken.
Love's not Time's fool, though rosy lips and cheeks
Within his bending sickle's compass come;
Love alters not with his brief hours and weeks,
But bears it out even to the edge of doom.
   If this be error and upon me proved,
    I never writ, nor no man ever loved.

SIR PHILIP SIDNEY

from *The Countess of Pembroke's Arcadia*

My true-love hath my hart, and I have his,
By just exchange one for the other giv'n.
I hold his dear, and mine he cannot miss:
There never was a better bargain driv'n.

His hart in me, keeps me and him in one;
My hart in him, his thoughts and senses guides:
He loves my hart, for once it was his own;
I cherish his, because in me it bides.

His hart his wound received from my sight;
My hart was wounded, with his wounded hart;
For as from me, on him his hurt did light,
So still me thought in me his hurt did smart:
Both equal hurt, in this change sought our bliss:
My true love hath my hart and I have his.

CAROL ANN DUFFY

White Writing

No vows written to wed you,
I write them white,
my lips on yours,
light in the soft hours of our married years.

No prayers written to bless you,
I write them white,
your soul a flame,
bright in the window of your maiden name.

No laws written to guard you,
I write them white,
your hand in mine,
palm against palm, lifeline, heartline.

No rules written to guide you,
I write them white,
words on the wind,
traced with a stick where we walk on the sand.

No news written to tell you,
I write it white,
foam on a wave
as we lift up our skirts in the sea, wade,

see last gold sun behind clouds,
inked water in moonlight.
No poems written to praise you,
I write them white.

DICK DAVIS

Uxor Vivamus . . .

The first night that I slept with you
And slept, I dreamt (these lines are true):
Now newly-married we had moved
Into an unkempt house we loved –
The rooms were large, the floors of stone,
The garden gently overgrown
With sunflowers, phlox, and mignonette –
All as we would have wished and yet
There was a shabby something there
Tainting the mild and windless air.
Where did it lurk? Alarmed we saw
The walls about us held the flaw –
They were of plaster, like grey chalk,
Porous and dead: it seemed our talk,
Our glances, even love, would die
With such indifference standing by.
Then, scarcely thinking what I did,
I chipped the plaster and it slid
In easy pieces to the floor;
It crumbled cleanly, more and more
Fell unresistingly away –
And there, beneath that deadening grey,
A fresco stood revealed: sky-blue
Predominated, for the view
Was an ebullient country scene,
The crowning of some pageant queen
Whose dress shone blue, and over all
The summer sky filled half the wall.
And so it was in every room,
The plaster's undistinguished gloom
Gave way to dances, festivals,
Processions, muted pastorals –
And everywhere that spacious blue:
I woke, and lying next to you
Knew all that I had dreamt was true.

ABRAHAM COWLEY

The Wish

Well then, I now do plainly see,
This busy world and I shall ne'er agree;
The very honey of all earthly joy
Does of all meats the soonest cloy.
And they, methinks, deserve my pity,
Who for it can endure the stings,
The Crowd, and Buzz, and Murmurings
Of this great Hive, the City.

Ah, yet, ere I descend to th' grave,
May I a small House and large Garden have!
And a few Friends, and many Books, both true,
Both wise, and both delightful too!
And since Love ne'er will from me flee,
A Mistress moderately fair,
And good as Guardian Angels are,
Only beloved and loving me!

O, Founts! O when in you shall I
Myself, eas'd of unpeaceful thoughts, espy?
O fields! O woods! when, when shall I be made
The happy Tenant of your shade?
Here's the spring-head of Pleasure's flood:
Here's wealthy Nature's treasury,
Where all the Riches lie that she
Has coin'd and stamp'd for good.

Pride and Ambition here
Only in far-fetch'd Metaphors appear;
Here nought but winds can hurtful Murmurs scatter,
And nought but Echo flatter.

The Gods, when they descend
From Heaven did always choose
And therefore we may boldly say
That 'tis the way too thither.

How happy here should I
And one dear She live, and embracing, die!
She who is all the world, and can exclude
In deserts solitude.
I should have then this only fear:
Lest men, when they my pleasures see,
Should hither throng to live like me,
And so make a City here.

PHILIP LARKIN

This Be The Verse

They fuck you up, your mum and dad.
    They may not mean to, but they do.
They fill you with the faults they had
    And add some extra, just for you.

But they were fucked up in their turn
    By fools in old-style hats and coats,
Who half the time were soppy-stern
    And half at one another's throats.

Man hands on misery to man.
    It deepens like a coastal shelf.
Get out as early as you can,
    And don't have any kids yourself.

he Worst

(... *sweet innocent thought that*
... *written: 'They tuck you up,*
... *um and dad'*)

... u up, your mum and dad,
... ou Peter Rabbit, too.
They gi.. you all the treats they had
And add some extra, just for you.

They were tucked up when they were small,
(Pink perfume, blue tobacco-smoke),
By those whose kiss healed any fall,
Whose laughter doubled any joke.

Man hands on happiness to man,
It deepens like a coastal shelf.
So love your parents all you can
And have some cheerful kids yourself.

Freight

I am the ship in which you sail,
little dancing bones,
your passage between the dream
and the waking dream,
your sieve, your pea-green boat.
I'll pay whatever toll your ferry needs.
And you, whose history's already charted
in a rope of cells, be tender to
those other unnamed vessels
who will surprise you one day,
tug-tugging, irresistible,
and float you out beyond your depth,
where you'll look down, puzzled, amazed.

MARK STRAND

'The Dreadful Has Already Happened'

The relatives are leaning over, staring expectantly.
They moisten their lips with their tongues. I can feel
them urging me on. I hold the baby in the air.
Heaps of broken bottles glitter in the sun.

A small band is playing old fashioned marches.
My mother is keeping time by stamping her foot.
My father is kissing a woman who keeps waving
to somebody else. There are palm trees.

The hills are spotted with orange flamboyants and tall
billowy clouds move behind them. 'Go on, Boy,'
I hear somebody say, 'Go on.'
I keep wondering if it will rain.

The sky darkens. There is thunder.
'Break his legs,' says one of my aunts,
'Now give him a kiss.' I do what I'm told.
The trees bend in the bleak tropical wind.

The baby did not scream, but I remember that sigh
when I reached inside for his tiny lungs and shook them
out in the air for the flies. The relatives cheered.
It was about that time I gave up.

Now, when I answer the phone, his lips
are in the receiver; when I sleep, his hair is gathered
around a familiar face on the pillow; wherever I search
I find his feet. He is what is left of my life.

WILLIAM WORDSWORTH

My heart leaps up when I behold
    A Rainbow in the sky:
So was it when my life began;
So is it now I am a Man;
So be it when I shall grow old,
    Or let me die!
The Child is Father of the Man;
And I could wish my days to be
Bound each to each by natural piety.

ROBERT BURNS

A Poet's Welcome to his love-begotten Daughter; the first instance that entitled him to the venerable appellation of Father

Thou 's welcome, Wean! Mischanter fa' me,
If thoughts o' thee, or yet thy Mamie,
Shall ever daunton me or awe me,
             My bonie lady;
Or if I blush when thou shalt name me
             Tyta, or Daddie. –

Tho' now they ca' me, Fornicator,
And tease my name in kintra clatter,
The mair they talk, I'm kend the better;
             E'en let them clash!
An auld wife's tongue 's a feckless matter
             To gie ane fash. –

Welcome! My bonie, sweet, wee Dochter!
Tho' ye come here a wee unsought for;
And tho' your comin I hae fought for,
             Baith Kirk and Queir;
Yet by my faith, ye're no unwrought for,
             That I shall swear!

Wee image o' my bonie Betty,
As fatherly I kiss and daut thee,
As dear and near my heart I set thee,
             Wi' as gude will,
As a' the Priests had seen me get thee
             That 's out o' h——. –

Wean child; *Mischanter* mishap; *daunton* subdue; *Tyta* informal name for father;
kintra clatter country gossip; *feckless* worthless; *daut* fondle

Sweet fruit o' monie a merry dint,
My funny toil is no a' tint;
Tho' ye come to the warld asklent,
                    Which fools may scoff at,
In my last plack your part 's be in 't,
                    The better half o't. –

Tho' I should be the waur bestead,
Tho 's be as braw and bienly clad,
And thy young years as nicely bred
                    Wi' education,
As any brat o' Wedlock's bed,
                    In a' thy station. –

Lord grant that thou may ay inherit
Thy Mither's looks an' gracefu' merit;
An' thy poor, worthless Daddie's spirit,
                    Without his failins!
'Twad please me mair to see thee heir it
                    Than stocked mailins!

For if thou be, what I wad hae thee,
And tak the counsel I shall gie thee,
I'll never rue my trouble wi' thee,
                    The cost nor shame o't,
But be a loving Father to thee,
                    And brag the name o't. –

tint lost; *asklent* on the side; *plack* coin; *waur bestead* worse placed; *braw* finely;
bienly warmly; *mailins* smallholdings

STEPHEN SPENDER

To My Daughter

Bright clasp of her whole hand around my finger,
My daughter, as we walk together now,
All my life I'll feel a ring invisibly
Circle this bone with shining: when she is grown
Far from today as her eyes are far already.

JAMES JOYCE

On the Beach at Fontana

Wind whines and whines the shingle,
The crazy pierstakes groan;
A senile sea numbers each single
Slimesilvered stone.

From whining wind and colder
Grey sea I wrap him warm
And touch his trembling fineboned shoulder
And boyish arm.

Around us fear, descending
Darkness of fear above
And in my heart how deep unending
Ache of love!

Trieste, 1914

GWEN HARWOOD

In the Park

She sits in the park. Her clothes are out of date.
Two children whine and bicker, tug her skirt.
A third draws aimless patterns in the dirt.
Someone she loved once passes by – too late

to feign indifference to that casual nod.
'How nice,' *et cetera*. 'Time holds great surprises.'
From his neat head unquestionably rises
a small balloon . . . 'but for the grace of God . . .'

They stand awhile in flickering light, rehearsing
the children's names and birthdays. 'It's so sweet
to hear their chatter, watch them grow and thrive,'
she says to his departing smile. Then, nursing
the youngest child, sits staring at her feet.
To the wind she says, 'They have eaten me alive.'

COVENTRY PATMORE

The Toys

My little Son, who look'd from thoughtful eyes
And moved and spoke in quiet grown-up wise,
Having my law the seventh time disobey'd,
I struck him, and dismiss'd
With hard words and unkiss'd,
His Mother, who was patient, being dead.
Then, fearing lest his grief should hinder sleep,
I visited his bed,
But found him slumbering deep,
With darken'd eyelids, and their lashes yet
From his late sobbing wet.
And I, with moan,
Kissing away his tears, left others of my own;
For, on a table drawn beside his head,
He had put, within his reach,
A box of counters and a red-vein'd stone,
A piece of glass abraded by the beach
And six or seven shells,
A bottle with bluebells
And two French copper coins, ranged there with
 careful art,
To comfort his sad heart.
So when that night I pray'd
To God, I wept, and said:
Ah, when at last we lie with tranced breath,
Not vexing Thee in death,
And Thou rememberest of what toys
We made our joys,
How weakly understood,
Thy great commanded good,
Then, fatherly not less
Than I whom Thou hast moulded from the clay,
Thou'lt leave Thy wrath, and say,
'I will be sorry for their childishness.'

CHARLES LAMB

Parental Recollections

A child's a plaything for an hour;
   Its pretty tricks we try
For that or for a longer space;
   Then tire, and lay it by.

But I knew one that to itself
   All seasons could control;
That would have mocked the sense of pain
   Out of a grievëd soul.

Thou straggler into loving arms,
   Young climber up of knees,
When I forget thy thousand ways,
   Then life and all shall cease.

FLEUR ADCOCK

For a Five-year-old

A snail is climbing up the window-sill
Into your room, after a night of rain.
You call me in to see, and I explain
That it would be unkind to leave it there:
It might crawl to the floor; we must take care
That no one squashes it. You understand,
And carry it outside, with careful hand,
To eat a daffodil.

I see, then, that a kind of faith prevails:
Your gentleness is moulded still by words
From me, who have trapped mice and shot wild birds,
From me, who drowned your kittens, who betrayed
Your closest relatives, and who purveyed
The harshest kind of truth to many another.
But that is how things are: I am your mother,
And we are kind to snails.

ROBIN ROBERTSON

New Gravity

Treading through the half-light of ivy
and headstone, I see you in the distance
as I'm telling our daughter
about this place, this whole business:
a sister about to be born,
how a life's new gravity suspends in water.
Under the oak, the fallen leaves
are pieces of the tree's jigsaw;
by your father's grave you are pressing acorns
into the shadows to seed.

BEN JONSON

On My First Son

Farewell, thou child of my right hand, and joy;
    My sin was too much hope of thee, lov'd boy.
Seven years thou wert lent to me, and I thee pay,
    Exacted by thy fate, on the just day.
Oh, could I lose all father, now. For why
    Will man lament the state he should envy?
To have so soon 'scaped world's and flesh's rage,
    And, if no other misery, yet age!
Rest in soft peace, and, ask'd, say, Here doth lie
    Ben Jonson his best piece of *poetry*.
For whose sake, hence-forth, all his vows be such,
    As what he loves may never like too much.

PEGGY CARR

Flight of the Firstborn

He streaks past his sixteenth year
small island life stretched tight
across his shoulders
his strides rehearsing city blocks
college brochures
airline schedules
stream excitedly through his
newly competent hands
his goodbyes like blurred neon
on a morning suddenly gone wet

I'm left stranded
on a tiny patch of time
still reaching
to wipe the cereal from his smile

ANNE BRADSTREET

In Reference to Her Children,
23 June, 1659

I had eight birds hatched in one nest,
Four cocks there were, and hens the rest.
I nursed them up with pain and care,
Nor cost, nor labour did I spare,
Till at the last they felt their wing,
Mounted the trees, and learned to sing;
Chief of the brood then took his flight
To regions far and left me quite.
My mournful chirps I after send,
Till he return, or I do end:
Leave not thy nest, thy dam and sire,
Fly back and sing amidst this choir.
My second bird did take her flight,
And with her mate flew out of sight;
Southward they both their course did bend,
And seasons twain they there did spend,
Till after blown by southern gales,
They norward steered with filled sails.
A prettier bird was no where seen,
Along the beach among the treen.
I have a third of colour white,
On whom I placed no small delight;
Coupled with mate loving and true,
Hath also bid her dam adieu;
And where Aurora first appears,
She now hath perched to spend her years.
One to the academy flew
To chat among that learned crew;
Ambition moves still in his breast
That he might chant above the rest,

Striving for more than to do well,
That nightingales he might excel.
My fifth, whose down is yet scarce gone,
Is 'mongst the shrubs and bushes flown,
And as his wings increase in strength,
On higher boughs he'll perch at length.
My other three still with me nest,
Until they're grown, then as the rest,
Or here or there they'll take their flight,
As is ordained, so shall they light.
If birds could weep, then would my tears
Let others know what are my fears
Lest this my brood some harm should catch,
And be surprised for want of watch,
Whilst pecking corn and void of care,
They fall un'wares in fowler's snare,
Or whilst on trees they sit and sing,
Some untoward boy at them do fling,
Or whilst allured with bell and glass,
The net be spread, and caught, alas.
Or lest by lime-twigs they be foiled,
Or by some greedy hawks be spoiled.
O would my young, ye saw my breast,
And knew what thoughts there sadly rest,
Great was my pain when I you bred,
Great was my care when I you fed,
Long did I keep you soft and warm,
And with my wings kept off all harm,
My cares are more and fears than ever,
My throbs such now as 'fore were never.
Alas, my birds, you wisdom want,
Of perils you are ignorant;
Oft times in grass, on trees, in flight,
Sore accidents on you may light.
O to your safety have an eye,
So happy may you live and die.
Meanwhile my days in tunes I'll spend,
Till my weak lays with me shall end.

In shady woods I'll sit and sing,
And things that past to mind I'll bring.
Once young and pleasant, as are you,
But former toys (no joys) adieu.
My age I will not once lament,
But sing, my time so near is spent.
And from the top bough take my flight
Into a country beyond sight,
Where old ones instantly grow young,
And there with seraphims set song;
No seasons cold, nor storms they see;
But spring lasts to eternity.
When each of you shall in your nest
Among your young ones take your rest,
In chirping language, oft them tell,
You had a dam that loved you well,
That did what could be done for young,
And nursed you up till you were strong,
And 'fore she once would let you fly,
She showed you joy and misery;
Taught what was good, and what was ill,
What would save life, and what would kill.
Thus gone, amongst you I may live,
And dead, yet speak, and counsel give:
Farewell, my birds, farewell adieu,
I happy am, if well with you.

WILLIAM CARLOS WILLIAMS

Danse Russe

If I when my wife is sleeping
and the baby and Kathleen
are sleeping
and the sun is a flame-white disc
in silken mists
above shining trees, –
if I in my north room
dance naked, grotesquely
before my mirror
waving my shirt round my head
and singing softly to myself:
'I am lonely, lonely.
I was born to be lonely,
I am best so!'
If I admire my arms, my face,
my shoulders, flanks, buttocks
against the yellow drawn shades, –

Who shall say I am not
the happy genius of my household?

ROBERT LOUIS STEVENSON

My house, I say. But hark to the sunny doves
That make my roof the arena of their loves,
That gyre about the gable all day long
And fill the chimneys with their murmurous song:
Our house, they say; and *mine*, the cat declares
And spreads his golden fleece upon the chairs;
And *mine* the dog, and rises stiff with wrath
If any alien foot profane the path.
So too the buck that trimmed my terraces,
Our whilome gardener, called the garden his;
Who now, deposed, surveys my plain abode
And his late kingdom, only from the road.

MICHAEL ONDAATJE

The Strange Case

My dog's assumed my alter ego.
Has taken over – walks the house
phallus hanging wealthy and raw
in front of guests, nuzzling
head up skirts
while I direct my mandarin mood.

Last week driving the baby sitter home.
She, unaware dog sat in the dark back seat,
talked on about the kids' behaviour.
On Huron Street the dog leaned forward
and licked her ear.
The car going 40 miles an hour
she seemed more amazed
at my driving ability
than my indiscretion.

It was only the dog I said.
Oh she said.
Me interpreting her reply all the way home.

DAVID CONSTANTINE

Don't jump off the roof, Dad . . .

I see the amplified mouths of my little ones
And dear old Betty beseeching me with a trowel.
I am the breadwinner, they want me down of course.
I expect they have telephoned the fire brigade.

They have misinterpreted my whizzing arms:
I am not losing my balance nor fighting wasps
Nor waving hello nor signalling for help.
These are my props and I am revving up.

From here I have pity on the whole estate.
The homegoing lollipop lady regards me with
        amazement.
I shall be on the news. Lovely Mrs Pemberton
Will clutch Mr Pemberton and cry: It's him!

Ladies, I am not bandy, it is the footing I must keep.
My run-up along the ridge-tiles will be inelegant.
But after lift-off, breasting the balmy wind
And when I bear westwards and have the wind in
        my tail

Then what a shot I shall make, going for the big sun,
Over the flowering cherries and the weeping willows,
Beating along Acacia Avenue with a purpose
Towards the park and the ornamental lake.

ROBERT BROWNING

Love in a Life

Room after room,
I hunt the house through
We inhabit together.
Heart, fear nothing, for, heart, thou shalt find her –
Next time, herself! – not the trouble behind her
Left in the curtain, the couch's perfume!
As she brushed it, the cornice-wreath blossomed anew:
Yon looking-glass gleamed at the wave of her feather.

Yet the day wears,
And door succeeds door;
I try the fresh fortune –
Range the wide house from the wing to the centre.
Still the same chance! she goes out as I enter.
Spend my whole day in the quest, – who cares?
But 'tis twilight, you see, – with such suites to explore,
Such closets to search, such alcoves to importune!

ROBERT CRAWFORD

Home

Has canary-yellow curtains, so expensive
At certain times they become unaffordable,
Cost too much patience. A cartoon voice:

'I'm leaving, Elmer.' That's home also, sometimes;
The Eden a person can't go back to. Still . . .
If you don't leave it, it's only a world;

If you never return, just a place like any other.
Home isn't in the *Blue Guide*, the A–Z
I only need for those ten thousand streets

Not one of which has Alice Wales in it.
At home you bolt on the new pine headboard,
Crying. You build from your tears

A hydroponicum; bitter-sweet nutrition
Becomes the address we ripen in like fruit
No one thought would grow here. Home

Is where we hang up our clothes and surnames
Without thought. Home is the instruction: dream
    home.
An architecture of faint clicks, and smells that
    haven't yet quite.

We grow old in it. Like children, it keeps us young,
Every evening being twenty-one again
With the key in the door, coming back from the
    library

You're shouting upstairs to me, telling me what
     you are
In the simplest of words, that I want you to go on
     repeating
Like a call-sign. You are shouting, 'I'm home.'

GRACE NICHOLS

Like a Beacon

In London
every now and then
I get this craving
for my mother's food
I leave art galleries
in search of plantains
saltfish/sweet potatoes

I need this link

I need this touch
of home
swinging my bag
like a beacon
against the cold

A. K. RAMANUJAN

Self-Portrait

I resemble everyone
but myself, and sometimes see
in shop-windows,
   despite the well-known laws
   of optics,
the portrait of a stranger,
date unknown,
often signed in a corner
by my father.

ROBERT HAYDEN

Those Winter Sundays

Sundays too my father got up early
and put his clothes on in the blueblack cold,
then with cracked hands that ached
from labor in the weekday weather made
banked fires blaze. No one ever thanked him.

I'd wake and hear the cold splintering, breaking.
When the rooms were warm, he'd call,
and slowly I would rise and dress,
fearing the chronic angers of that house,

Speaking indifferently to him,
who had driven out the cold
and polished my good shoes as well.
What did I know, what did I know
of love's austere and lonely offices?

DILIP CHITRE

Father Returning Home

My father travels on the late evening train
Standing among silent commuters in the yellow light
Suburbs slide past his unseeing eyes
His shirt and pants are soggy and his black raincoat
Stained with mud and his bag stuffed with books
Is falling apart. His eyes dimmed by age
Fade homeward through the humid monsoon night.
Now I can see him getting off the train
Like a word dropped from a long sentence.
He hurries across the length of the grey platform.
Crosses the railway line, enters the lane,
His chappals are sticky with mud, but he hurries
     onward.

Home again, I see him drinking weak tea,
Eating a stale chapati, reading a book.
He goes into the toilet to contemplate
Man's estrangement from a man-made world.
Coming out he trembles at the sink,
The cold water running over his brown hands,
A few droplets cling to the greying hairs on his wrists.
His sullen children have often refused to share
Jokes and secrets with him. He will now go to sleep
Listening to the static on the radio, dreaming
Of his ancestors and grandchildren, thinking
Of nomads entering a subcontinent through a narrow
     pass.

VINCENT BUCKLEY

from *Stroke*

At the merest handshake I feel his blood
Move with the ebb-tide chill. Who can revive
A body settled in its final mood?
To whom, on what tide, can we move, and live?

Later I wheel him out to see the trees:
Willows and oaks, the small plants he mistakes
For rose bushes; and there
In the front, looming, light green, cypresses.
His pulse no stronger than the pulse of air.

Dying, he grows more tender, learns to teach
Himself the mysteries I am left to trace.
As I bend to say 'Till next time', I search
For signs of resurrection in his face.

ELIZABETH JENNINGS

One Flesh

Lying apart now, each in a separate bed,
He with a book, keeping the light on late,
She like a girl dreaming of childhood,
All men elsewhere – it is as if they wait
Some new event: the book he holds unread,
Her eyes fixed on the shadows overhead.

Tossed up like flotsam from a former passion,
How cool they lie. They hardly ever touch,
Or if they do it is like a confession
Of having little feeling – or too much.
Chastity faces them, a destination
For which their whole lives were a preparation.

Strangely apart, yet strangely close together,
Silence between them like a thread to hold
And not wind in. And time itself's a feather
Touching them gently. Do they know they're old,
These two who are my father and my mother
Whose fire from which I came, has now grown cold?

ANNE FINCH, COUNTESS OF WINCHILSEA

The Unequal Fetters

Cou'd we stop the time that's flying
   Or recall it when 'tis past
Put far off the day of Dying
   Or make Youth for ever last
To Love wou'd then be worth our cost.

But since we must lose those Graces
   Which at first your hearts have won
And you seek for in new Faces
   When our Spring of Life is done
It wou'd but urge our ruin on

Free as Nature's first intention
   Was to make us, I'll be found
Nor by subtle Man's invention
   Yield to be in Fetters bound
By one that walks a freer round.

Marriage does but slightly tie Men
   Whil'st close Pris'ners we remain
They the larger Slaves of Hymen
   Still are begging Love again
At the full length of all their chain.

CHARLOTTE MEW

The Farmer's Bride

Three Summers since I chose a maid –
Too young maybe – but more's to do
At harvest-time than bide and woo.
    When us was wed she turned afraid
Of love and me and all things human;
Like the shut of a winter's day
Her smile went out, and 'twasn't a woman –
    More like a little frightened fay.
        One night, in the Fall, she runned away.

'Out 'mong the sheep, her be,' they said,
'Should properly have been abed;
But sure enough she wasn't there
Lying awake with her wide brown stare.
So over seven-acre field and up-along across the
        down
We chased her, flying like a hare
Before our lanterns. To Church-Town
    All in a shiver and a scare
We caught her, fetched her home at last,
    And turned the key upon her, fast.

She does the work about the house
As well as most, but like a mouse.
    Happy enough to chat and play
    With birds and rabbits and such as they,
    So long as men-folk keep away.
'Not near, not near!' her eyes beseech
When one of us comes within reach.
    The women say that beasts in stall
    Look round like children at her call.
    I've hardly heard her speak at all.

Shy as a leveret, swift as he,
Straight and slight as a young larch tree,
Sweet as the first wild violets, she,
To her wild self. But what to me?

The short days shorten, and the oaks are brown,
    The blue smoke rises to the low grey sky,
One leaf in the still air falls slowly down,
    A magpie's spotted feathers lie
On the black earth spread white with rime,
The berries redden up to Christmas-time.
    What's Christmas-time without there be
    Some other in the house than we!

    She sleeps up in the attic there
    Alone, poor maid. 'Tis but a stair
Betwixt us. Oh! my God! the down,
    The soft young down of her, the brown,
The brown of her – her eyes, her hair, her hair!

GEOFFREY CHAUCER

from The Wife of Bath's Prologue in *The Canterbury Tales*

'Now sire, thanne wol I telle yow forth my tale.
As evere moot I drinken win or ale,
I shal seye sooth: tho housbondes that I hadde,
As three of hem were goode, and two were badde.
The thre men were goode, and riche, and olde.
Unnethe mighte they the statut holde
In which that they were bounden unto me –
Ye woot wel what I mene of this, pardee!
As help me God, I laughe whan I thinke
How pitously a-night I made hem swinke.
And by my fey, I tolde of it no stoor.
They hadde me yeven hir land and hir tresoor;
Me neded nat do lenger diligence
To winne hir love, or doon hem reverence.
They loved me so wel, by God above,
That I ne tolde no deintee of hir love.
A wis womman wol bisye hire evere in oon
To gete hir love, ye, theras she hath noon.
But sith I hadde hem hoolly in min hond,
And sith they hadde me yeven al hir lond,
What sholde I taken kepe hem for to plese,
But it were for my profit and min ese?
I sette hem so a-werke, by my fey,
That many a night they songen 'weilawey!'
The bacon was nat fet for hem, I trowe,
That som men han in Essex at Donmowe.

moot must; *sooth* truth; *hem* them; *Unnethe mighte they the statut holde* with difficulty could they fulfil the obligation; *woot* know; *swinke* labour; *fey* faith; *tolde of it no stoor* set no store by it; *yeven* given; *doon hem reverence* show them respect; *ne tolde no deintee* set no store by; *bisye hire* exert herself; *taken kepe* be concerned; *But* unless; *a-werke* to work; *fet* fetched

I governed hem so wel after my lawe,
That ech of hem ful blisful was and fawe
To bringe me gaye thinges fro the feire.
They were ful glad whan I spak to hem feire,
For God it woot, I chidde hem spitously.
   'Now herkneth how I bar me proprely.
Ye wise wives that konne understonde,
Thus sholde ye speke and bere hem wrong on honde,
For half so boldely kan ther no man
Sweren and lien as a womman kan.
I sey nat this by wives that ben wise,
But if it be whan they hem misavise.
A wis wif, if that she kan hir good,
Shal beren him on hond the cow is wood,
And take witnesse of hir owene maide
Of hir assent – but herkneth how I saide.'

fawe eager; *feire* fair; *feire* kindly; *spitously* mercilessly; *bar me proprely* behaved
characteristically; *bere hem wrong on honde* make false allegations against them;
hem misavise are misguided; *kan hir good* knows what's to her advantage; *beren*
him on hond swear to him; *wood* mad; *Of hir assent* with her connivance;
herkneth hear

WILLIAM SHAKESPEARE

from *The Winter's Tale*, I, ii

LEONTES (*aside*):

                             Too hot, too hot!
To mingle friendship far is mingling bloods.
I have *tremor cordis* on me: my heart dances,
But not for joy, not joy. This entertainment
May a free face put on, derive a liberty
From heartiness, from bounty, fertile bosom,
And well become the agent – 't may, I grant.
But to be paddling palms and pinching fingers,
As now they are, and making practised smiles
As in a looking glass; and then to sigh, as 'twere
The mort o'th'deer – O, that is entertainment
My bosom likes not, nor my brows!

                *   *   *

                   Ha'not you seen, Camillo –
But that's past doubt, you have, or your eye-glass
Is thicker than a cuckold's horn – or heard –
For to a vision so apparent rumour
Cannot be mute – or thought – for cogitation
Resides not in that man that does not think –
My wife is slippery? If thou wilt confess –
Or else be impudently negative
To have nor eyes, nor ears, nor thought – then say
My wife's a hobby-horse, deserves a name
As rank as any flax-wench that puts to
Before her troth-plight: say't and justify't.

CAMILLO:

I would not be a stander-by to hear
My sovereign mistress clouded so without
My present vengeance taken. 'Shrew my heart,
You never spoke what did become you less

Than this; which to reiterate were sin
As deep as that, though true.
LEONTES:

                              Is whispering nothing?
Is leaning cheek to cheek? Is meeting noses?
Kissing with inside lip? Stopping the career
Of laughter with a sigh? – a note infallible
Of breaking honesty. Horsing foot on foot?
Skulking in corners? Wishing clocks more swift?
Hours minutes? Noon midnight? And all eyes
Blind with the pin and web but theirs, theirs only,
That would unseen be wicked – is this nothing?
Why, then the world and all that's in't is nothing;
The covering sky is nothing; Bohemia nothing;
My wife is nothing; nor nothing have these nothings,
If this be nothing.

GEORGE GORDON, LORD BYRON
from *Don Juan*, Canto III

V

'Tis melancholy and a fearful sign
  Of human frailty, folly, also crime,
That love and marriage rarely can combine,
  Although they both are born in the same clime.
Marriage from love, like vinegar from wine –
  A sad, sour, sober beverage – by time
Is sharpened from its high celestial flavour
Down to a very homely household savour.

VI

There's something of antipathy, as 'twere,
  Between their present and their future state.
A kind of flattery that's hardly fair
  Is used until the truth arrives too late.
Yet what can people do, except despair?
  The same things change their names at such a rate;
For instance, passion in a lover's glorious,
But in a husband is pronounced uxorious.

VII

Men grow ashamed of being so very fond;
  They sometimes also get a little tired
(But that, of course, is rare) and then despond.
  The same things cannot always be admired,
Yet 'tis 'so nominated in the bond'
  That both are tied till one shall have expired.
Sad thought! to lose the spouse that was adorning
Our days, and put one's servants into mourning.

VIII

There's doubtless something in domestic doings,
   Which forms in fact true love's antithesis.
Romances paint at full length people's wooings,
   But only give a bust of marriages,
For no one cares for matrimonial cooings;
   There's nothing wrong in a connubial kiss.
Think you, if Laura had been Petrarch's wife,
He would have written sonnets all his life?

EZRA POUND

The Bath Tub

As a bathtub lined with white porcelain,
When the hot water gives out or goes tepid,
So is the slow cooling of our chivalrous passion,
O my much praised but-not-altogether-satisfactory lady.

JOHN MILTON

from *Paradise Lost*, Book IX

They sat them down to weep, nor only tears
Rained at their eyes, but high winds worse within
Began to rise, high passions, anger, hate,
Mistrust, suspicion, discord, and shook sore
Their inward state of mind, calm region once
And full of peace, now tossed and turbulent:
For understanding ruled not, and the will
Heard not her lore, both in subjection now
To sensual appetite, who from beneath
Usurping over sov'reign reason claimed
Superior sway: from thus distempered breast,
Adam, estranged in look and altered style,
Speech intermitted thus to Eve renewed.
    Would thou hadst hearkened to my words, and
        stayed
With me, as I besought thee, when that strange
Desire of wand'ring this unhappy morn,
I know not whence possessed thee; we had then
Remained still happy, not as now, despoiled
Of all our good, shamed, naked, miserable.
Let none henceforth seek needless cause to approve
The faith they owe; when earnestly they seek
Such proof, conclude, they then begin to fail.
    To whom soon moved with touch of blame thus Eve.
What words have passed thy lips, Adam severe,
Imput'st thou that to my default, or will
Of wand'ring, as thou call'st it, which who knows
But might as ill have happened thou being by,
Or to thyself perhaps: hadst thou been there,
Or here th' attempt, thou couldst not have discerned
Fraud in the serpent, speaking as he spake;
No ground of enmity between us known,
Why he should mean me ill, or seek to harm.

Was I to have never parted from thy side?
As good have grown there still a lifeless rib.
Being as I am, why didst not thou the head
Command me absolutely not to go,
Going into such danger as thou saidst?
Too facile then thou didst not much gainsay,
Nay, didst permit, approve, and fair dismiss.
Hadst thou been firm and fixed in thy dissent,
Neither had I transgressed, nor thou with me.
   To whom then first incensed Adam replied.
Is this the love, is this the recompense
Of mine to thee, ingrateful Eve, expressed
Immutable when thou wert lost, not I,
Who might have lived and joyed immortal bliss,
Yet willingly chose rather death with thee:
And am I now upbraided, as the cause
Of thy transgressing? not enough severe,
It seems, in thy restraint: what could I more?
I warned thee, I admonished thee, foretold
The danger, and the lurking Enemy
That lay in wait; beyond this had been force,
And force upon free will hath here no place.
But confidence then bore thee on, secure
Either to meet no danger, or to find
Matter of glorious trial, and perhaps
I also erred in overmuch admiring
What seemed in thee so perfect, that I thought
No evil durst attempt thee, but I rue
That error now, which is become my crime,
And thou th' accuser. Thus it shall befall
Him who to worth in women overtrusting
Lets her will rule; restraint she will not brook,
And left to herself, if evil thence ensue,
She first his weak indulgence will accuse.
   Thus they in mutual accusation spent
The fruitless hours, but neither self-condemning,
And of their vain contest appeared no end.

GEORGE MEREDITH

from *Modern Love*

XVII

At dinner she is hostess, I am host.
Went the feast ever cheerfuller? She keeps
The Topic over intellectual deeps
In buoyancy afloat. They see no ghost.
With sparkling surface-eyes we ply the ball:
It is in truth a most contagious game;
HIDING THE SKELETON shall be its name.
Such play as this the devils might appal!
But here's the greater wonder; in that we,
Enamour'd of our acting and our wits,
Admire each other like true hypocrites.
Warm-lighted glances, Love's Ephemerae,
Shoot gaily o'er the dishes and the wine.
We waken envy of our happy lot.
Fast, sweet, and golden, shows our marriage-knot.
Dear guests, you now have seen Love's corpse-light
     shine!

PATIENCE AGBABI

Accidentally Falling

Cheers
to the not
so distant
past They
always say
the first
sip is the
accidentally
falling in
lust period
Had we never
met each other
happened to fall
together entwined
I would not vintage
that bitter-sweet taste of
lips met over a glass of wine
experience ninesummersrolled
deliciously into our one green
bottle Caressed by the waves
we went the way of all lovers
when tipsy swaying to the hum of
summer bees our lust dried up
ran through fingers like sand
We noticed one-another's faults
your eyes took on that half-empty
half-hearted all is over look
You laughed when my jokes were
serious I cried when we were
bodily united mentally untied
tossing on a grey pebble beach
desperate scraping the barrel
making it up only to quarrel
making nothing but memories
drew the whole thing out until
it was out of control finished
sentimental dust I relive it
annually smiling vacant over
a bottle of wine now it's over
past just like the other nine

ERNEST DOWSON

Non Sum Qualis Eram Bonae Sub Regno Cynarae

Last night, ah, yesternight, betwixt her lips and mine
There fell thy shadow, Cynara! thy breath was shed
Upon my soul between the kisses and the wine;
And I was desolate and sick of an old passion,
    Yea, I was desolate and bowed my head:
I have been faithful to thee, Cynara! in my fashion.

All night upon mine heart I felt her warm heart beat,
Night-long within mine arms in love and sleep she lay;
Surely the kisses of her bought red mouth were sweet;
But I was desolate and sick of an old passion,
    When I awoke and found the dawn was gray:
I have been faithful to thee, Cynara! in my fashion.

I have forgot much, Cynara! gone with the wind,
Flung roses, roses riotously with the throng,
Dancing, to put thy pale, lost lilies out of mind;
But I was desolate and sick of an old passion,
    Yea, all the time, because the dance was long:
I have been faithful to thee, Cynara! in my fashion.

I cried for madder music and for stronger wine,
But when the feast is finished and the lamps expire,
Then falls thy shadow, Cynara! the night is thine;
And I am desolate and sick of an old passion,
    Yea, hungry for the lips of my desire:
I have been faithful to thee, Cynara! in my fashion.

JOHN DRYDEN

from *Marriage A-La-Mode*, I, i

Why should a foolish Marriage Vow
    Which long ago was made,
Oblige us to each other now
    When Passion is decay'd?
We lov'd, and we lov'd, as long as we cou'd,
    Till our love was lov'd out in us both:
But our Marriage is dead, when the Pleasure
      is fled:
    'Twas Pleasure first made it an Oath.

If I have Pleasures for a Friend,
    And farther love in store,
What wrong has he whose joys did end,
    And who cou'd give no more?
'Tis a madness that he should be jealous of me,
    Or that I shou'd bar him of another:
For all we can gain, is to give our selves pain,
    When neither can hinder the other.

MICHAEL DRAYTON

Since there's no help, come let us kiss and part:
Nay, I have done; You get no more of Me,
And I am glad, yea glad with all my heart,
That thus so cleanly I my self can free.
Shake hands for ever, cancel all our Vows,
And when we meet at any time again,
Be it not seen in either of our Brows
That we one jot of former Love retain.
Now at the last gasp of Love's latest Breath,
When, his Pulse failing, Passion speechless lies,
When Faith is kneeling by his bed of Death
And Innocence is closing up his Eyes;
    Now, if thou would'st, when all have given him over,
    From Death to Life thou might'st him yet recover.

SIR THOMAS WYATT

They flee from me, that sometime did me seek
With naked Foot stalking within my Chamber.
Once have I seen them gentle, tame, and meek,
That now are wild, and do not once remember
That sometime they have put themselves in danger
To take Bread at my Hand; and now they range
Busily seeking with a continual change.

Thanked be Fortune, it hath been otherwise
Twenty Times better; but once in special,
In thin Array, after a pleasant guise,
When her loose Gown did from her Shoulders fall
And she me caught in her Arms long and small,
And therewithal sweetly did me kiss,
And softly said, 'Dear heart, how like you this?'

It was no Dream; for I lay broad waking:
But all is turned thorough my gentleness,
Into a strange Fashion of forsaking;
And I have leave to go of her goodness
And she also to use new fangleness.
But since that I so kindly am served
I would fain know what hath she deserved.

NICK LAIRD

To The Wife

After this iceblink and sudden death of the mammals –
that wolfhound our youngest will poison with gravy on
    sponges,
the calf whose back leg you fatally shatter, driving home
    fast,
too sad, from the clinic – and after neither of us have a
    mother
or father and we've washed up our minuscule five o'clock
    dinners,

having pottered around the stores all afternoon, mumbling,
buttonholing assistants to complain about prices or rain,
and change over our eyewear to examine the papers
with that contemptuous squint we'll both have adopted,
and decide how we've read all the books that we will,
and think even those in the end offered hassle and pain,

do you think we could find a way back to an evening
when holding each other will not be about balance
and all of the tunes are inside us and wordless?

D. H. LAWRE[N]

Trust

Oh we've got to trust
one another again
in some essentials.

Not the narrow little
bargaining trust
that says: I'm for you
if you'll be for me. –

But a bigger trust,
a trust of the sun
that does not bother
about moth and rust,
and we see it shining
in one another.

Oh don't you trust me,
don't burden me
with your life and affairs; don't
        thrust me
into your cares.

But I think you may trust
the sun in me
that glows with just
as much glow as you see
in me, and no more.

But if it warms
your heart's quick core
why then trust it, it forms
one faithfulness more.

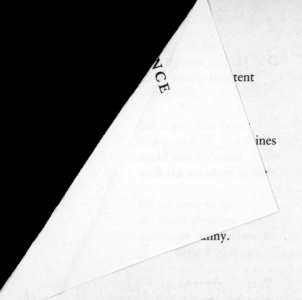

tent

ines

nny.

WILLIAM SHAKESPEARE

Sonnet 18

Shall I compare thee to a summer's day?
Thou art more lovely and more temperate.
Rough winds do shake the darling buds of May,
And summer's lease hath all too short a date.
Sometimes too hot the eye of heaven shines,
And often is his gold complexion dimmed;
And every fair from fair sometimes declines,
By chance or nature's changing course untrimmed.
But thy eternal summer shall not fade,
Nor lose possession of that fair thou ow'st,
Nor shall Death brag thou wand'rest in his shade,
When in eternal lines to time thou grow'st.
   So long as men can breathe or eyes can see,
   So long lives this, and this gives life to thee.

DOUGLAS DUNN

Modern Love

It is summer, and we are in a house
That is not ours, sitting at a table
Enjoying minutes of a rented silence,
The upstairs people gone. The pigeons lull
To sleep the under-tens and invalids,
The tree shakes out its shadows to the grass,
The roses rove through the wilds of my neglect.
Our lives flap, and we have no hope of better
Happiness than this, not much to show for love
But how we are, or how this evening is,
Unpeopled, silent, and where we are alive
In a domestic love, seemingly alone,
All other lives worn down to trees and sunlight,
Looking forward to a visit from the cat.

SEAMUS HEANEY

The Skunk

Up, black, striped and damasked like the chasuble
At a funeral mass, the skunk's tail
Paraded the skunk. Night after night
I expected her like a visitor.

The refrigerator whinnied into silence.
My desk light softened beyond the veranda.
Small oranges loomed in the orange tree.
I began to be tense as a voyeur.

After eleven years I was composing
Love-letters again, broaching the word 'wife'
Like a stored cask, as if its slender vowel
Had mutated into the night earth and air

Of California. The beautiful, useless
Tang of eucalyptus spelt your absence.
The aftermath of a mouthful of wine
Was like inhaling you off a cold pillow.

And there she was, the intent and glamorous,
Ordinary, mysterious skunk,
Mythologized, demythologized,
Snuffing the boards five feet beyond me.

It all came back to me last night, stirred
By the sootfall of your things at bedtime,
Your head-down, tail-up hunt in a bottom drawer
For the black plunge-line nightdress.

THOM GUNN

The Hug

It was your birthday, we had drunk and dined
    Half of the night with our old friend
        Who'd showed us in the end
    To a bed I reached in one drunk stride.
      Already I lay snug,
And drowsy with the wine dozed on one side.

I dozed, I slept. My sleep broke on a hug,
    Suddenly, from behind,
In which the full lengths of our bodies pressed:
    Your instep to my heel,
  My shoulder-blades against your chest.
  It was not sex, but I could feel
  The whole strength of your body set,
    Or braced, to mine,
    And locking me to you
  As if we were still twenty-two
  When our grand passion had not yet
    Become familial.
  My quick sleep had deleted all
  Of intervening time and place.
    I only knew
The stay of your secure firm dry embrace.

ANNE BRADSTREET

To My Dear and Loving Husband

If ever two were one, then surely we.
If ever man were loved by wife, then thee;
If ever wife was happy in a man,
Compare with me, ye women, if you can.
I prize thy love more than whole mines of gold
Or all the riches that the East doth hold.
My love is such that rivers cannot quench,
Nor ought but love from thee, give recompense.
Thy love is such I can no way repay,
The heavens reward thee manifold, I pray.
Then while we live, in love let's so persevere
That when we live no more, we may live ever.

GEORGE CRABBE

The ring so worn, as you behold,
So thin, so pale, is yet of gold:
The passion such it was to prove;
Worn with life's cares, love yet was love.

DOM MORAES

Future Plans

Absorbed with each other's flesh
In the tumbled beds of our youth,
We had conversations with children
Not born to us yet, but named.
Those faculties, now disrupted,
Shed selves, must exist somewhere,
As they did when our summer ended:
Leela-Claire, and the first death.
Mark, cold on a hospital tray
At five months: I was away then
With tribesmen in bronze forests.
We became our children, my wife.
Now, left alone with each other,
As we were in four continents,
At the turn of your classic head,
At your private smile, the beacon
You beckon with, I recall them.
We may travel there once more.
We shall leave at the proper time,
As a couple, without complaint,
With a destination in common
And some regrets and memories.
We shall leave in ways we believed
Impossible in our youth,
A little tired, but in the end,
Not unhappy to have lived.

JOHN DONNE

Love's Growth

I scarce believe my love to be so pure
    As I had thought it was,
    Because it doth endure
Vicissitude, and season, as the grass;
Methinks I lied all winter, when I swore,
My love was infinite, if spring make it more.
But if this medicine, love, which cures all sorrow
With more, not only be no quintessence,
But mixed of all stuffs, paining soul, or sense,
And of the sun his working vigour borrow,
Love's not so pure, and abstract, as they use
To say, which have no mistress but their Muse,
But as all else, being elemented too,
Love sometimes would contemplate, sometimes do.

And yet not greater, but more eminent,
    Love by the spring is grown;
    As, in the firmament,
Stars by the sun are not enlarged, but shown,
Gentle love deeds, as blossoms on a bough,
From love's awakened root do bud out now.
If, as in water stirred more circles be
Produced by one, love such additions take,
Those like so many spheres, but one heaven make,
For, they are all concentric unto thee,
And though each spring do add to love new heat,
As princes do in times of action get
New taxes, and remit them not in peace,
No winter shall abate the spring's increase.

Getting Older,
Looking Back

ALISON FELL

Pushing forty

Just before winter
we see the trees show
their true colours:
the mad yellow of chestnuts
two maples like blood sisters
the orange beech
braver than lipstick

Pushing forty, we vow
that when the time comes
rather than wither
ladylike and white
we will henna our hair
like Colette, we too
will be gold and red
and go out
in a last wild blaze

JOHN KEATS

To Autumn

Season of mists and mellow fruitfulness,
   Close bosom-friend of the maturing sun;
Conspiring with him how to load and bless
   With fruit the vines that round the thatch-eves run;
To bend with apples the moss'd cottage-trees,
   And fill all fruit with ripeness to the core;
     To swell the gourd, and plump the hazel shells
With a sweet kernel; to set budding more,
   And still more, later flowers for the bees,
   Until they think warm days will never cease,
     For Summer has o'er-brimm'd their clammy cells.

Who hath not seen thee oft amid thy store?
   Sometimes whoever seeks abroad may find
Thee sitting careless on a granary floor,
   Thy hair soft-lifted by the winnowing wind;
Or on a half-reap'd furrow sound asleep,
   Drows'd with the fume of poppies, while thy hook
     Spares the next swath and all its twined flowers:
And sometimes like a gleaner thou dost keep
   Steady thy laden head across a brook;
   Or by a cyder-press, with patient look,
     Thou watchest the last oozings hours by hours.

Where are the songs of Spring? Ay, where are they?
   Think not of them, thou hast thy music too –
While barred clouds bloom the soft-dying day,
   And touch the stubble-plains with rosy hue;
Then in a wailful choir the small gnats mourn
   Among the river sallows, borne aloft
     Or sinking as the light wind lives or dies;
And full-grown lambs loud bleat from hilly bourn;
   Hedge-crickets sing; and now with treble soft
   The red-breast whistles from a garden-croft;
     And gathering swallows twitter in the skies.

ANDREW MARVELL

The Garden

How vainly men themselves amaze
To win the palm, the oak, or bays,
And their uncessant labours see
Crowned from some single herb or tree,
Whose short and narrow-vergèd shade
Does prudently their toils upbraid;
While all flow'rs and all trees do close
To weave the garlands of repose.

Fair Quiet, have I found thee here,
And Innocence thy sister dear!
Mistaken long, I sought you then
In busy companies of men.
Your sacred plants, if here below,
Only among the plants will grow.
Society is all but rude,
To this delicious solitude.

No white nor red was ever seen
So am'rous as this lovely green.
Fond lovers, cruel as their flame,
Cut in these trees their mistress' name.
Little, alas, they know or heed
How far these beauties hers exceed!
Fair trees! Wheres'e'er your barks I wound,
No name shall but your own be found.

When we have run our passions' heat
Love hither makes his best retreat.
The gods, that mortal beauty chase,
Still in a tree did end their race:
Apollo hunted Daphne so,
Only that she might laurel grow;
And Pan did after Syrinx speed,
Not as a nymph, but for a reed.

What wondrous life is this I lead!
Ripe apples drop about my head;
The luscious clusters of the vine
Upon my mouth do crush their wine;
The nectarine and curious peach
Into my hands themselves do reach.
Stumbling on melons, as I pass,
Ensnared with flow'rs, I fall on grass.

Meanwhile the mind, from pleasure less
Withdraws into its happiness:
The mind, that ocean where each kind
Does straight its own resemblance find;
Yet it creates, transcending these,
Far other worlds, and other seas;
Annihilating all that's made
To a green thought in a green shade.

Here at the fountain's sliding foot
Or at some fruit-tree's mossy root,
Casting the body's vest aside,
My soul into the boughs does glide.
There like a bird it sits and sings,
Then whets and combs its silver wings;
And, till prepared for longer flight,
Waves in its plumes the various light.

Such was that happy garden-state,
While man there walked without a mate:
After a place so pure and sweet,
What other help could yet be meet?
But 'twas beyond a mortal's share
To wander solitary there:
Two paradises 'twere in one
To live in paradise alone.

How well the skilful gard'ner drew
Of flow'rs and herbs this dial new;
Where from above the milder sun
Does through a fragrant zodiac run;
And, as it works, th' industrious bee
Computes its time as well as we.
How could such sweet and wholesome hours
Be reckoned but with herbs and flow'rs?

FREDERICK GODDARD TUCKERMAN

As when down some broad river dropping, we
Day after day behold the assuming shores
Sink and grow dim, as the great watercourse
Pushes his banks apart and seeks the sea:
Benches of pines, high shelf and balcony,
To flats of willow and low sycamores
Subsiding, till where'er the wave we see,
Himself is his horizon utterly.
So fades the portion of our early world,
Still on the ambit hangs the purple air;
Yet while we lean to read the secret there,
The stream that by green shoresides plashed and
    purled
Expands: the mountains melt to vapors rare,
And life alone circles out flat and bare.

MATTHEW ARNOLD

Dover Beach

The sea is calm to-night.
The tide is full, the moon lies fair
Upon the straits; – on the French coast the light
Gleams and is gone; the cliffs of England stand,
Glimmering and vast, out in the tranquil bay.
Come to the window, sweet is the night-air!
Only, from the long line of spray
Where the sea meets the moon-blanch'd land,
Listen! you hear the grating roar
Of pebbles which the waves draw back, and fling,
At their return, up the high strand,
Begin, and cease, and then again begin,
With tremulous cadence slow, and bring
The eternal note of sadness in.

Sophocles long ago
Heard it on the Aegaean, and it brought
Into his mind the turbid ebb and flow
Of human misery; we
Find also in the sound a thought,
Hearing it by this distant northern sea.

The Sea of Faith
Was once, too, at the full, and round earth's shore
Lay like the folds of a bright girdle furl'd.
But now I only hear
Its melancholy, long, withdrawing roar,
Retreating, to the breath
Of the night-wind, down the vast edges drear
And naked shingles of the world.

Ah, love, let us be true
To one another! for the world, which seems
To lie before us like a land of dreams,
So various, so beautiful, so new,
Hath really neither joy, nor love, nor light,
Nor certitude, nor peace, nor help for pain;
And we are here as on a darkling plain
Swept with confused alarms of struggle and flight,
Where ignorant armies clash by night.

JOHN CLARE

'I Am'

I am – yet what I am, none cares or knows;
    My friends forsake me like a memory lost: –
I am the self-consumer of my woes; –
    They rise and vanish in oblivion's host,
Like shadows in love's frenzied stifled throes: –
And yet I am, and live – like vapours tost

Into the nothingness of scorn and noise, –
    Into the living sea of waking dreams,
Where there is neither sense of life or joys,
    But the vast shipwreck of my life's esteems;
Even the dearest, that I love the best
Are strange – nay, rather stranger than the rest.

I long for scenes, where man hath never trod
    A place where woman never smiled or wept
There to abide with my Creator, God;
    And sleep as I in childhood, sweetly slept,
Untroubling, and untroubled where I lie,
The grass below – above, the vaulted sky.

HENRY WADSWORTH LONGFELLOW

Mezzo Cammin

Half of my life is gone, and I have let
   The years slip from me and have not fulfilled
   The aspiration of my youth, to build
   Some tower of song with lofty parapet.
Not indolence, nor pleasure, nor the fret
   Of restless passions that would not be stilled,
   But sorrow, and a care that almost killed,
   Kept me from what I may accomplish yet;
Though, half-way up the hill, I see the Past
   Lying beneath me with its sounds and sights, –
   A city in the twilight dim and vast,
With smoking roofs, soft bells, and gleaming lights, –
   And hear above me on the autumnal blast
   The cataract of Death far thundering from the heights.

PHILIP LARKIN

The Old Fools

What do they think has happened, the old fools,
To make them like this? Do they somehow suppose
It's more grown-up when your mouth hangs open and drools,
And you keep on pissing yourself, and can't remember
Who called this morning? Or that, if they only chose,
They could alter things back to when they danced all night,
Or went to their wedding, or sloped arms some September?
Or do they fancy there's really been no change,
And they've always behaved as if they were crippled or tight,
Or sat through days of thin continuous dreaming
Watching light move? If they don't (and they can't), it's
      strange:
        Why aren't they screaming?

At death, you break up: the bits that were you
Start speeding away from each other for ever
With no one to see. It's only oblivion, true:
We had it before, but then it was going to end,
And was all the time merging with a unique endeavour
To bring to bloom the million-petalled flower
Of being here. Next time you can't pretend
There'll be anything else. And these are the first signs:
Not knowing how, not hearing who, the power
Of choosing gone. Their looks show that they're for it:
Ash hair, toad hands, prune face dried into lines –
        How can they ignore it?

Perhaps being old is having lighted rooms
Inside your head, and people in them, acting.
People you know, yet can't quite name; each looms
Like a deep loss restored, from known doors turning,

Setting down a lamp, smiling from a stair, extracting
A known book from the shelves; or sometimes only
The rooms themselves, chairs and a fire burning,
The blown bush at the window, or the sun's
Faint friendliness on the wall some lonely
Rain-ceased midsummer evening. That is where they live:
Not here and now, but where all happened once.
          This is why they give

An air of baffled absence, trying to be there
Yet being here. For the rooms grow farther, leaving
Incompetent cold, the constant wear and tear
Of taken breath, and them crouching below
Extinction's alp, the old fools, never perceiving
How near it is. This must be what keeps them quiet:
The peak that stays in view wherever we go
For them is rising ground. Can they never tell
What is dragging them back, and how it will end? Not at
          night?
Not when the strangers come? Never, throughout
The whole hideous inverted childhood? Well,
          We shall find out.

Grayheaded Schoolchildren

Old men have bad dreams,
So they sleep little.
They walk on bare feet
Without turning on the lights,
Or they stand leaning
On gloomy furniture
Listening to their hearts beat.

The one window across the room
Is black like a blackboard.
Every old man is alone
In this classroom, squinting
At that fine chalk line
That divides being-here
From being-here-no-more.

No matter. It was a glass of water
They were going to get,
But not just yet.
They listen for mice in the walls,
A car passing on the street,
Their dead fathers shuffling past them
On their way to the kitchen.

ROBERT SOUTHEY

The Old Man's Comforts and How He Gained Them

You are old, Father William, the young man cried,
  The few locks which are left you are grey;
You are hale, Father William, a hearty old man,
  Now tell me the reason, I pray.

In the days of my youth, Father William replied,
  I remember'd that youth would fly fast,
And abused not my health and my vigour at first,
  That I never might need them at last.

You are old, Father William, the young man cried,
  And pleasures with youth pass away;
And yet you lament not the days that are gone,
  Now tell me the reason, I pray.

In the days of my youth, Father William replied,
  I remember'd that youth could not last;
I thought of the future, whatever I did,
  That I never might grieve for the past.

You are old, Father William, the young man cried,
  And life must be hastening away;
You are cheerful, and love to converse upon death,
  Now tell me the reason, I pray.

I am cheerful, young man, Father William replied,
  Let the cause thy attention engage;
In the days of my youth I remember'd my God!
  And He hath not forgotten my age.

from *Alice's Adventures in Wonderland*

'You are old, Father William,' the young man said,
　'And your hair has become very white;
And yet you incessantly stand on your head –
　Do you think, at your age, it is right?'

'In my youth,' Father William replied to his son,
　'I feared it might injure the brain;
But, now that I'm perfectly sure I have none,
　Why, I do it again and again.'

'You are old,' said the youth, 'as I mentioned before,
　And have grown most uncommonly fat;
Yet you turned a back-somersault in at the door –
　Pray, what is the reason of that?'

'In my youth,' said the sage, as he shook his grey locks,
　'I kept all my limbs very supple
By the use of this ointment – one shilling the box –
　Allow me to sell you a couple?'

'You are old,' said the youth, 'and your jaws are too weak
　For anything tougher than suet;
Yet you finished the goose, with the bones and the beak –
　Pray, how did you manage to do it?'

'In my youth,' said his father, 'I took to the law,
　And argued each case with my wife;
And the muscular strength, which it gave to my jaw
　Has lasted the rest of my life.'

'You are old,' said the youth, 'one would hardly suppose
    That your eye was as steady as ever;
Yet you balanced an eel on the end of your nose –
    What made you so awfully clever?'

'I have answered three questions, and that is enough,'
    Said his father. 'Don't give yourself airs!
Do you think I can listen all day to such stuff?
    Be off, or I'll kick you down-stairs!'

T. S. ELIOT

The Love Song of J. Alfred Prufrock

*S'io credessi che mia risposta fosse
a persona che mai tornasse al mondo,
questa fiamma staria senza più scosse.
Ma per ciò che giammai di questo fondo
non tornò vivo alcun, s'i' odo il vero,
senza tema d'infamia ti rispondo.*

  Let us go then, you and I,
When the evening is spread out against the sky
Like a patient etherised upon a table;
Let us go, through certain half-deserted streets,
The muttering retreats
Of restless nights in one-night cheap hotels
And sawdust restaurants with oyster-shells:
Streets that follow like a tedious argument
Of insidious intent
To lead you to an overwhelming question . . .
Oh, do not ask, 'What is it?'
Let us go and make our visit.

  In the room the women come and go
Talking of Michelangelo.

  The yellow fog that rubs its back upon the window-panes,
The yellow smoke that rubs its muzzle on the window-panes,
Licked its tongue into the corners of the evening,
Lingered upon the pools that stand in drains,
Let fall upon its back the soot that falls from chimneys,
Slipped by the terrace, made a sudden leap,
And seeing that it was a soft October night,
Curled once about the house, and fell asleep.

And indeed there will be time
For the yellow smoke that slides along the street
Rubbing its back upon the window-panes;
There will be time, there will be time
To prepare a face to meet the faces that you meet;
There will be time to murder and create,
And time for all the works and days of hands
That lift and drop a question on your plate;
Time for you and time for me,
And time yet for a hundred indecisions,
And for a hundred visions and revisions,
Before the taking of a toast and tea.

In the room the women come and go
Talking of Michelangelo.

And indeed there will be time
To wonder, 'Do I dare?' and, 'Do I dare?'
Time to turn back and descend the stair,
With a bald spot in the middle of my hair –
(They will say: 'How his hair is growing thin!')
My morning coat, my collar mounting firmly to
        the chin,
My necktie rich and modest, but asserted by a
        simple pin –
(They will say: 'But how his arms and legs are thin!')
Do I dare
Disturb the universe?
In a minute there is time
For decisions and revisions which a minute will reverse.

For I have known them all already, known them all –
Have known the evenings, mornings, afternoons,
I have measured out my life with coffee spoons;
I know the voices dying with a dying fall
Beneath the music from a farther room.
    So how should I presume?

And I have known the eyes already, known them all –
The eyes that fix you in a formulated phrase,
And when I am formulated, sprawling on a pin,
When I am pinned and wriggling on the wall,
Then how should I begin
To spit out all the butt-ends of my days and ways?
 And how should I presume?

 And I have known the arms already, known them all –
Arms that are braceleted and white and bare
(But in the lamplight, downed with light brown hair!)
Is it perfume from a dress
That makes me so digress?
Arms that lie along a table, or wrap about a shawl.
 And should I then presume?
 And how should I begin?

 .   .   .   .   .

 Shall I say, I have gone at dusk through narrow streets
And watched the smoke that rises from the pipes
Of lonely men in shirt-sleeves, leaning out of windows? . . .

 I should have been a pair of ragged claws
Scuttling across the floors of silent seas.

 .   .   .   .   .

 And the afternoon, the evening, sleeps so peacefully!
Smoothed by long fingers,
Asleep . . . tired . . . or it malingers,
Stretched on the floor, here beside you and me.
Should I, after tea and cakes and ices,
Have the strength to force the moment to its crisis?
But though I have wept and fasted, wept and prayed,
Though I have seen my head (grown slightly bald) brought
 in upon a platter,
I am no prophet – and here's no great matter;
I have seen the moment of my greatness flicker,
And I have seen the eternal Footman hold my coat, and
 snicker,
And in short, I was afraid.

And would it have been worth it, after all,
After the cups, the marmalade, the tea,
Among the porcelain, among some talk of you and me,
Would it have been worth while,
To have bitten off the matter with a smile,
To have squeezed the universe into a ball
To roll it towards some overwhelming question,
To say: 'I am Lazarus, come from the dead,
Come back to tell you all, I shall tell you all' –
If one, settling a pillow by her head,
    Should say: 'That is not what I meant at all.
    That is not it, at all.'

    And would it have been worth it, after all,
Would it have been worth while,
After the sunsets and the dooryards and the sprinkled
       streets,
After the novels, after the teacups, after the skirts that
       trail along the floor –
And this, and so much more? –
It is impossible to say just what I mean!
But as if a magic lantern threw the nerves in patterns
       on a screen:
Would it have been worth while
If one, settling a pillow or throwing off a shawl,
And turning toward the window, should say:
    'That is not it at all,
    That is not what I meant, at all.'
     .   .   .   .   .

    No! I am not Prince Hamlet, nor was meant to be;
Am an attendant lord, one that will do
To swell a progress, start a scene or two,
Advise the prince; no doubt, an easy tool,
Deferential, glad to be of use,
Politic, cautious, and meticulous;
Full of high sentence, but a bit obtuse;
At times, indeed, almost ridiculous –
Almost, at times, the Fool.

I grow old . . . I grow old . . .
I shall wear the bottoms of my trousers rolled.

Shall I part my hair behind? Do I dare to eat a peach?
I shall wear white flannel trousers, and walk upon the beach.
I have heard the mermaids singing, each to each.

I do not think that they will sing to me.

I have seen them riding seaward on the waves
Combing the white hair of the waves blown back
When the wind blows the water white and black.

We have lingered in the chambers of the sea
By sea-girls wreathed with seaweed red and brown
Till human voices wake us, and we drown.

RALPH WALDO EMERSON

Terminus

It is time to be old,
To take in sail: –
The god of bounds,
Who sets to seas a shore,
Came to me in his fatal rounds,
And said: 'No more!
No farther spread
Thy broad ambitious branches, and thy root.
Fancy departs: no more invent,
Contract thy firmament
To compass of a tent.
There's not enough for this and that,
Make thy option which of two;
Economize the failing river,
Not the less revere the Giver,
Leave the many and hold the few.
Timely wise accept the terms,
Soften the fall with wary foot;
A little while
Still plan and smile,
And, fault of novel germs,
Mature the unfallen fruit.
Curse, if thou wilt, thy sires,
Bad husbands of their fires,
Who, when they gave thee breath,
Failed to bequeath
The needful sinew stark as once,
The Baresark marrow to thy bones,
But left a legacy of ebbing veins,
Inconstant heat and nerveless reins, –
Amid the Muses, left thee deaf and dumb,
Amid the gladiators, halt and numb.'

As the bird trims her to the gale,
I trim myself to the storm of time,
I man the rudder, reef the sail,
Obey the voice at eve obeyed at prime:
'Lowly faithful, banish fear,
Right onward drive unharmed;
The port, well worth the cruise, is near,
And every wave is charmed.'

W. B. YEATS

Sailing to Byzantium

That is no country for old men. The young
In one another's arms, birds in the trees
– Those dying generations – at their song,
The salmon-falls, the mackerel-crowded seas,
Fish, flesh, or fowl, commend all summer long
Whatever is begotten, born, and dies.
Caught in that sensual music all neglect
Monuments of unageing intellect.

An aged man is but a paltry thing,
A tattered coat upon a stick, unless
Soul clap its hands and sing, and louder sing
For every tatter in its mortal dress,
Nor is there singing school but studying
Monuments of its own magnificence;
And therefore I have sailed the seas and come
To the holy city of Byzantium.

O sages standing in God's holy fire
As in the gold mosaic of a wall,
Come from the holy fire, perne in a gyre,
And be the singing-masters of my soul.
Consume my heart away; sick with desire
And fastened to a dying animal
It knows not what it is; and gather me
Into the artifice of eternity.

Once out of nature I shall never take
My bodily form from any natural thing,
But such a form as Grecian goldsmiths make
Of hammered gold and gold enamelling

To keep a drowsy Emperor awake;
Or set upon a golden bough to sing
To lords and ladies of Byzantium
Of what is past, or passing, or to come.

CAROLE SATYAMURTI

Day Trip

Two women, seventies, hold hands
on the edge of Essex,
hair in strong nets,
shrieked laughter echoing gulls
as shingle sucks from under feet
easing in brine.

There must be an unspoken point
when the sea feels like
their future. No longer paddling,
ankles submerge in lace,
in satin ripple.
Dress hems darken.

They do not risk their balance
for the shimmering of ships
at the horizon's sweep
as, thigh deep, they inch on
fingers splayed, wrists bent,
learning to walk again.

JENNY JOSEPH

Warning

When I am an old woman I shall wear purple
With a red hat which doesn't go, and doesn't suit me.
And I shall spend my pension on brandy and summer
    gloves
And satin sandals, and say we've no money for butter.
I shall sit down on the pavement when I'm tired
And gobble up samples in shops and press alarm bells
And run my stick along the public railings
And make up for the sobriety of my youth.
I shall go out in my slippers in the rain
And pick the flowers in other people's gardens
And learn to spit.

You can wear terrible shirts and grow more fat
And eat three pounds of sausages at a go
Or only bread and pickle for a week
And hoard pens and pencils and beermats and things in
    boxes.

But now we must have clothes that keep us dry
And pay our rent and not swear in the street
And set a good example for the children.
We must have friends to dinner and read the papers.

But maybe I ought to practise a little now?
So people who know me are not too shocked and
    surprised
When suddenly I am old, and start to wear purple.

WOLE SOYINKA

To My First White Hairs

Hirsute hell chimney-spouts, black thunderthroes
confluence of coarse cloudfleeces – my head sir! –
    scourbrush
in bitumen, past fossil beyond fingers of light – until . . . !

Sudden sprung as corn stalk after rain, watered milk weak;
as lightning shrunk to ant's antenna, shrivelled
off the febrile sight of crickets in the sun –

THREE WHITE HAIRS! frail invaders of the
    undergrowth
interpret time. I view them, wired wisps, vibrant coiled
beneath a magnifying glass, milk-thread presages

Of the hoary phase. Weave then, weave o quickly weave
your sham veneration. Knit me webs of winter sagehood,
nightcap, and the fungoid sequins of a crown.

ALFRED, LORD TENNYSON

Ulysses

It little profits that an idle king,
By this still hearth, among these barren crags,
Matched with an agèd wife, I mete and dole
Unequal laws unto a savage race,
That hoard, and sleep, and feed, and know not me.

I cannot rest from travel: I will drink
Life to the lees: all times I have enjoyed
Greatly, have suffered greatly, both with those
That loved me, and alone; on shore, and when
Through scudding drifts the rainy Hyades
Vext the dim sea: I am become a name;
For always roaming with a hungry heart
Much have I seen and known; cities of men
And manners, climates, councils, governments,
Myself not least, but honoured of them all;
And drunk delight of battle with my peers,
Far on the ringing plains of windy Troy.
I am a part of all that I have met;
Yet all experience is an arch wherethrough
Gleams that untravelled world, whose margin fades
For ever and for ever when I move.
How dull it is to pause, to make an end,
To rust unburnished, not to shine in use!
As though to breathe were life. Life piled on life
Were all too little, and of one to me
Little remains: but every hour is saved
From that eternal silence, something more,
A bringer of new things; and vile it were
For some three suns to store and hoard myself,
And this gray spirit yearning in desire
To follow knowledge like a sinking star,
Beyond the utmost bound of human thought.

This is my son, mine own Telemachus,
To whom I leave the sceptre and the isle –
Well-loved of me, discerning to fulfil
This labour, by slow prudence to make mild
A rugged people, and through soft degrees
Subdue them to the useful and the good.
Most blameless is he, centred in the sphere
Of common duties, decent not to fail
In offices of tenderness, and pay
Meet adoration to my household gods,
When I am gone. He works his work, I mine.

There lies the port; the vessel puffs her sail:
There gloom the dark broad seas. My mariners,
Souls that have toiled, and wrought, and thought with me –
That ever with a frolic welcome took
The thunder and the sunshine, and opposed
Free hearts, free foreheads – you and I are old;
Old age hath yet his honour and his toil;
Death closes all: but something ere the end,
Some work of noble note, may yet be done,
Not unbecoming men that strove with Gods.
The lights begin to twinkle from the rocks:
The long day wanes: the slow moon climbs: the deep
Moans round with many voices. Come, my friends,
'Tis not too late to seek a newer world.
Push off, and sitting well in order smite
The sounding furrows; for my purpose holds
To sail beyond the sunset, and the baths
Of all the western stars, until I die.
It may be that the gulfs will wash us down:
It may be we shall touch the Happy Isles,
And see the great Achilles, whom we knew.
Though much is taken, much abides; and though
We are not now that strength which in old days
Moved earth and heaven; that which we are, we are;
One equal temper of heroic hearts,
Made weak by time and fate, but strong in will
To strive, to seek, to find, and not to yield.

SIR HENRY LEE

His Golden locks, Time hath to Silver turn'd,
O Time too swift, O Swiftness never ceasing:
His Youth 'gainst Time and Age hath ever spurn'd,
But spurn'd in vain; Youth waneth by increasing.
   Beauty, Strength, Youth, are flowers but fading seen;
   Duty, Faith, Love, are roots, and ever green.

His helmet now, shall make a hive for Bees;
And Lovers' Sonnets turn'd to holy Psalms,
A man at Arms must now serve on his knees,
And feed on prayers, which are Age his alms:
   But though from Court to Cottage he depart,
   His Saint is sure of his unspotted heart.

And when he saddest sits in homely Cell,
He'll teach his Swains this Carol for a Song,
Blessed be the hearts that wish my Sovereign well,
Cursed be the souls that think her any wrong.
   Goddess, allow this agèd man his right
   To be your Beads-man now, that was your Knight.

JOHN MILTON

When I consider how my light is spent,
   Ere half my days, in this dark world and wide,
   And that one talent which is death to hide,
   Lodged with me useless, though my soul more bent
To serve therewith my Maker, and present
   My true account, lest he returning chide,
   Doth God exact day labour, light denied,
   I fondly ask; but patience to prevent
That murmur, soon replies, God doth not need
   Either man's work or his own gifts; who best
   Bear his mild yoke, they serve him best; his state
Is kingly. Thousands at his bidding speed
   And post o'er land and ocean without rest:
   They also serve who only stand and wait.

GEORGE HERBERT

The Forerunners

The harbingers are come. See, see their mark;
White is their colour, and behold my head.
But must they have my brain? must they dispark
Those sparkling notions, which therein were bred?
       Must dullness turn me to a clod?
Yet have they left me, *Thou art still my God*.

Good men ye be, to leave me my best room,
Ev'n all my heart, and what is lodged there:
I pass not, I, what of the rest become,
So *Thou art still my God*, be out of fear.
       He will be pleased with that ditty;
And if I please him, I write fine and witty.

Farewell sweet phrases, lovely metaphors.
But will ye leave me thus? when ye before
Of stews and brothels only knew the doors,
Then did I wash you with my tears, and more,
       Brought you to Church well dress'd and clad:
My God must have my best, ev'n all I had.

Lovely enchanting language, sugar-cane,
Honey of roses, whither wilt thou fly?
Hath some fond lover tic'd thee to thy bane?
And wilt thou leave the Church, and love a sty?
       Fie, thou wilt soil thy broider'd coat,
And hurt thyself, and him that sings the note.

Let foolish lovers, if they will love dung,
And canvas, not with arras, clothe their shame:
Let folly speak in her own native tongue.
True beauty dwells on high: ours is a flame
        But borrow'd thence to light us thither.
Beauty and beauteous words should go together.

Yet if you go, I pass not; take your way:
For, *Thou art still my God*, is all that ye
Perhaps with more embellishment can say,
Go birds of spring: let winter have his fee,
        Let a bleak paleness chalk the door,
So all within be livelier than before.

WILLIAM WORDSWORTH

Old Man Travelling

Animal Tranquillity and Decay, A Sketch

The little hedge-row birds,
That peck along the road, regard him not.
He travels on, and in his face, his step,
His gait, is one expression; every limb,
His look and bending figure, all bespeak
A man who does not move with pain, but moves
With thought – He is insensibly subdued
To settled quiet: he is one by whom
All effort seems forgotten, one to whom
Long patience has such mild composure given,
That patience now doth seem a thing, of which
He hath no need. He is by nature led
To peace so perfect, that the young behold
With envy, what the old man hardly feels.
– I asked him whither he was bound, and what
The object of his journey; he replied
'Sir! I am going many miles to take
A last leave of my son, a mariner,
Who from a sea-fight has been brought to Falmouth,
And there is dying in an hospital.'

JAMES HENRY

Very Old Man

I well remember how some threescore years
And ten ago, a helpless babe, I toddled
From chair to chair about my mother's chamber,
Feeling, as 'twere, my way in the new world
And foolishly afraid of, or, as 't might be,
Foolishly pleased with, th' unknown objects round me.
And now with stiffened joints I sit all day
In one of those same chairs, as foolishly
Hoping or fearing something from me hid
Behind the thick, dark veil which I see hourly
And minutely on every side round closing
And from my view all objects shutting out.

EDWARD THOMAS

Old Man

Old Man, or Lad's-love, – in the name there's nothing
To one that knows not Lad's-love, or Old Man,
The hoar-green feathery herb, almost a tree,
Growing with rosemary and lavender.
Even to one that knows it well, the names
Half decorate, half perplex, the thing it is:
At least, what that is clings not to the names
In spite of time. And yet I like the names.

The herb itself I like not, but for certain
I love it, as some day the child will love it
Who plucks a feather from the door-side bush
Whenever she goes in or out of the house.
Often she waits there, snipping the tips and
    shrivelling
The shreds at last on to the path, perhaps
Thinking, perhaps of nothing, till she sniffs
Her fingers and runs off. The bush is still
But half as tall as she, though it is as old;
So well she clips it. Not a word she says;
And I can only wonder how much hereafter
She will remember, with that bitter scent,
Of garden rows, and ancient damson-trees
Topping a hedge, a bent path to a door,
A low thick bush beside the door, and me
Forbidding her to pick.

           As for myself,
Where first I met the bitter scent is lost.
I, too, often shrivel the grey shreds,
Sniff them and think and sniff again and try
Once more to think what it is I am remembering,

Always in vain. I cannot like the scent,
Yet I would rather give up others more sweet,
With no meaning, than this bitter one.

I have mislaid the key. I sniff the spray
And think of nothing; I see and I hear nothing;
Yet seem, too, to be listening, lying in wait
For what I should, yet never can, remember:
No garden appears, no path, no hoar-green bush
Of Lad's-love, or Old Man, no child beside,
Neither father nor mother, nor any playmate;
Only an avenue, dark, nameless, without end.

MATTHEW ARNOLD
Growing Old

What is it to grow old?
Is it to lose the glory of the form,
The lustre of the eye?
Is it for beauty to forego her wreath?
– Yes, but not this alone.

Is it to feel our strength –
Not our bloom only, but our strength – decay?
Is it to feel each limb
Grow stiffer, every function less exact,
Each nerve more loosely strung?

Yes, this, and more; but not
Ah, 'tis not what in youth we dream'd 'twould be!
'Tis not to have our life
Mellow'd and soften'd as with sunset-glow,
A golden day's decline.

'Tis not to see the world
As from a height, with rapt prophetic eyes,
And heart profoundly stirr'd;
And weep, and feel the fulness of the past,
The years that are no more.

It is to spend long days
And not once feel that we were ever young;
It is to add, immured
In the hot prison of the present, month
To month with weary pain.

It is to suffer this,
And feel but half, and feebly, what we feel.
Deep in our hidden heart
Festers the dull remembrance of a change,
But no emotion – none.

It is – last stage of all –
When we are frozen up within, and quite
The phantom of ourselves,
To hear the world applaud the hollow ghost
Which blamed the living man.

STEPHEN SPENDER

What I expected, was
Thunder, fighting,
Long struggles with men
And climbing.
After continual straining
I should grow strong;
Then the rocks would shake,
And I rest long.

What I had not foreseen
Was the gradual day
Weakening the will
Leaking the brightness away,
The lack of good to touch,
The fading of body and soul
– Smoke before wind,
Corrupt, unsubstantial.

The wearing of Time,
And the watching of cripples pass
With limbs shaped like questions
In their odd twist,
The pulverous grief
Melting the bones with pity,
The sick falling from earth –
These, I could not foresee.

Expecting always
Some brightness to hold in trust,
Some final innocence
Exempt from dust,
That, hanging solid,
Would dangle through all,
Like the created poem,
Or faceted crystal.

T. E. HULME

The Embankment

(The fantasia of a fallen gentleman on a cold, bitter night)

Once, in finesse of fiddles found I ecstasy,
In the flash of gold heels on the hard pavement.
Now see I
That warmth's the very stuff of poesy.
Oh, God, make small
The old star-eaten blanket of the sky,
That I may fold it round me and in comfort lie.

ERNEST DOWSON

Vitae summa brevis spem nos vetat incohare longam

They are not long, the weeping and the laughter
    Love and desire and hate:
I think they have no portion in us after
    We pass the gate.

They are not long, the days of wine and roses:
    Out of a misty dream
Our path emerges for a while, then closes
    Within a dream.

W. B. YEATS
When You are Old

When you are old and grey and full of sleep,
And nodding by the fire, take down this book,
And slowly read, and dream of the soft look
Your eyes had once, and of their shadows deep;

How many loved your moments of glad grace,
And loved your beauty with love false or true,
But one man loved the pilgrim soul in you,
And loved the sorrows of your changing face;

And bending down beside the glowing bars,
Murmur, a little sadly, how Love fled
And paced upon the mountains overhead
And hid his face amid a crowd of stars.

STEVIE SMITH
Pad, pad

I always remember your beautiful flowers
And the beautiful kimono you wore
When you sat on the couch
With that tigerish crouch
And told me you loved me no more.

What I cannot remember is how I felt when you were
    unkind
All I know is, if you were unkind now I should not mind.
Ah me, the power to feel exaggerated, angry and sad
The years have taken from me. Softly I go now, pad pad.

A Song of a Young Lady.
To her Ancient Lover

Ancient person, for whom I
All the flattering youth defy,
Long be it ere thou grow old,
Aching, shaking, crazy, cold.
But still continue as thou art,
Ancient person of my heart.

On thy withered lips and dry,
Which like barren furrows lie,
Brooding kisses I will pour
Shall thy youthful heat restore,
Such kind showers in autumn fall
And a second spring recall,
Nor from thee will ever part,
Ancient person of my heart.

Thy nobler part, which but to name
In our sex would be counted shame,
By Age's frozen grasp possessed,
From his ice shall be released,
And, soothed by my reviving hand,
In former warmth and vigour stand.
All a lover's wish can reach,
For thy joy my love shall teach.

And for thy pleasure shall improve
All that art can add to love.
Yet still I love thee without art,
Ancient person of my heart.

LEIGH HUNT

Rondeau

Jenny kissed me when we met,
   Jumping from the chair she sat in;
Time, you thief, who love to get
   Sweets into your list, put that in:
Say I'm weary, say I'm sad,
   Say that health and wealth have missed me,
Say I'm growing old, but add,
   Jenny kissed me.

WILLIAM SHAKESPEARE

Sonnet 73

That time of year thou mayst in me behold
When yellow leaves, or none, or few, do hang
Upon those boughs which shake against the cold,
Bare ruined choirs where late the sweet birds sang.
In me thou seest the twilight of such day
As after sunset fadeth in the west,
Which by and by black night doth take away,
Death's second self, that seals up all in rest.
In me thou seest the glowing of such fire
That on the ashes of his youth doth lie,
As the deathbed whereon it must expire,
Consumed with that which it was nourished by.
  This thou perceiv'st, which makes thy love more
     strong,
  To love that well which thou must leave ere long.

ROBERT BURNS

John Anderson My Jo

John Anderson my jo, John,
When we were first acquent;
Your locks were like the raven,
Your bony brow was brent;
But now your brow is beld, John,
Your locks are like the snaw;
But blessings on your frosty pow,
John Anderson my jo.

John Anderson my jo, John,
We clamb the hill the gither;
And mony a canty day, John,
We've had wi' ane anither:
Now we maun totter down, John,
And hand in hand we'll go:
And sleep the gither at the foot,
John Anderson my jo.

jo dear; *acquent* acquainted; *brent* smooth; *beld* bald; *pow* head; *the gither*
together; *canty* pleasant; *maun* must

GEORGE GORDON, LORD BYRON

So, we'll go no more a roving
   So late into the night,
Though the heart be still as loving,
   And the moon be still as bright.

For the sword outwears its sheath,
   And the soul wears out the breast,
And the heart must pause to breathe,
   And love itself have rest.

Though the night was made for loving,
   And the day returns too soon,
Yet we'll go no more a roving
   By the light of the moon.

THOMAS MOORE

Oft, in the stilly night,
    Ere Slumber's chain has bound me,
Fond Memory brings the light
    Of other days around me;
        The smiles, the tears,
        Of boyhood's years,
    The words of love then spoken;
        The eyes that shone,
        Now dimm'd and gone,
    The cheerful hearts now broken!
Thus, in the stilly night,
    Ere Slumber's chain has bound me,
Sad Memory brings the light
    Of other days around me.

When I remember all
    The friends, so link'd together,
I've seen around me fall,
    Like leaves in wintry weather;
        I feel like one
        Who treads alone
    Some banquet-hall deserted,
        Whose lights are fled,
        Whose garland's dead,
    And all but he departed!
Thus in the stilly night,
    Ere Slumber's chain has bound me,
Sad Memory brings the light
    Of other days around me.

EDWARD THOMAS

Adlestrop

Yes. I remember Adlestrop –
The name, because one afternoon
Of heat the express-train drew up there
Unwontedly. It was late June.

The steam hissed. Someone cleared his throat.
No one left and no one came
On the bare platform. What I saw
Was Adlestrop – only the name

And willows, willow-herb, and grass,
And meadowsweet, and haycocks dry,
No whit less still and lonely fair
Than the high cloudlets in the sky.

And for that minute a blackbird sang
Close by, and round him, mistier,
Farther and farther, all the birds
Of Oxfordshire and Gloucestershire.

ALGERNON CHARLES SWINBURNE

A Vision of Spring in Winter

O tender time that love thinks long to see,
   Sweet foot of spring that with her footfall sows
   Late snowlike flowery leavings of the snows,
Be not too long irresolute to be;
O mother-month, where have they hidden thee?
   Out of the pale time of the flowerless rose
I reach my heart out toward the springtime lands,
   I stretch my spirit forth to the fair hours,
     The purplest of the prime:
I lean my soul down over them, with hands
   Made wide to take the ghostly growths of flowers:
     I send my love back to the lovely time.

Where has the greenwood hid thy gracious head?
   Veiled with what visions while the grey world grieves,
   Or muffled with what shadows of green leaves,
What warm intangible green shadows spread
To sweeten the sweet twilight for thy bed?
   What sleep enchants thee? what delight deceives?
Where the deep dreamlike dew before the dawn
   Feels not the fingers of the sunlight yet
     Its silver web unweave,
Thy footless ghost on some unfooted lawn
   Whose air the unrisen sunbeams fear to fret
     Lives a ghost's life of daylong dawn and eve.

Sunrise it sees not, neither set of star,
   Large nightfall, nor imperial plenilune,
   Nor strong sweet shape of the full-breasted noon;
But where the silver-sandalled shadows are,
Too soft for arrows of the sun to mar,

Moves with the mild gait of an ungrown moon:
Hard overhead the half-lit crescent swims,
　　The tender-coloured night draws hardly breath,
　　　The light is listening;
They watch the dawn of slender-shapen limbs,
　　Virginal, born again of doubtful death,
　　　Chill foster-father of the weanling spring.

As sweet desire of day before the day,
　　As dreams of love before the true love born,
　　From the outer edge of winter overworn
The ghost arisen of May before the May
Takes through dim air her unawakened way,
　　The gracious ghost of morning risen ere morn.
With little unblown breasts and child-eyed looks
　　Following, the very maid, the girl-child spring,
　　　Lifts windward her bright brows,
Dips her light feet in warm and moving brooks,
　　And kindles with her own mouth's colouring
　　　The fearful firstlings of the plumeless boughs.

I seek thee sleeping, and awhile I see,
　　Fair face that art not, how thy maiden breath
　　Shall put at last the deadly days to death
And fill the fields and fire the woods with thee
And seaward hollows where my feet would be
　　When heaven shall hear the word that April saith
To change the cold heart of the weary time,
　　To stir and soften all the time to tears,
　　　Tears joyfuller than mirth;
As even to May's clear height the young days climb
　　With feet not swifter than those fair first years
　　　Whose flower revive not with thy flowers on earth.

I would not bid thee, though I might, give back
　　One good thing youth has given and borne away;
　　I crave not any comfort of the day
That is not, nor on time's retrodden track
Would turn to meet the white-robed hours or black

That long since left me on their mortal way;
Nor light nor love that has been, nor the breath
   That comes with morning from the sun to be
      And sets light hope on fire;
No fruit, no flower thought once too fair for death,
   No flower nor hour once fallen from life's green tree,
      No leaf once plucked or once fulfilled desire.

The morning song beneath the stars that fled
   With twilight through the moonless mountain air,
   While youth with burning lips and wreathless hair
Sang toward the sun that was to crown his head,
Rising; the hopes that triumphed and fell dead,
   The sweet swift eyes and songs of hours that were;
These may'st thou not give back for ever; these,
   As at the sea's heart all her wrecks lie waste,
      Lie deeper than the sea;
But flowers thou may'st, and winds, and hours of ease,
   And all its April to the world thou may'st
      Give back, and half my April back to me.

THOMAS HOOD

I Remember, I Remember

I remember, I remember,
The house where I was born,
The little window where the sun
Came peeping in at morn;
He never came a wink too soon,
Nor brought too long a day,
But now, I often wish the night
Had borne my breath away!

I remember, I remember,
The roses, red and white,
The vi'lets, and the lily-cups,
Those flowers made of light!
The lilacs where the robin built,
And where my brother set
The liburnam on his birth-day, –
The tree is living yet!

I remember, I remember
Where I was used to swing,
And thought the air must rush as fresh
To swallows on the wing;
My spirit flew in feathers then,
That is so heavy now,
And summer pools could hardly cool
The fever on my brow!

I remember, I remember
The fir trees dark and high;
I used to think their slender tops
Were close against the sky:

It was a childish ignorance,
But now 'tis little joy
To know I'm farther off from heav'n
Than when I was a boy.

D. H. LAWRENCE

Piano

Softly, in the dusk, a woman is singing to me
Taking me back down the vista of years, till I see
A child sitting under the piano, in the boom of the
    tingling strings
And pressing the small, poised feet of a mother who
    smiles as she sings.

In spite of myself, the insidious mastery of song
Betrays me back, till the heart of me weeps to belong
To the old Sunday evenings at home, with winter outside
And hymns in the cosy parlour, the tinkling piano our
    guide.

So now it is vain for the singer to burst into clamour
With the great black piano appassionato. The glamour
Of childish days is upon me, my manhood is cast
Down in the flood of remembrance, I weep like a child
    for the past.

WILLIAM SHAKESPEARE

Sonnet 30

When to the sessions of sweet silent thought
I summon up remembrance of things past,
I sigh the lack of many a thing I sought,
And with old woes new wail my dear time's waste;
Then can I drown an eye, unused to flow,
For precious friends hid in death's dateless night,
And weep afresh love's long since cancelled woe,
And moan th'expense of many a vanished sight;
Then can I grieve at grievances foregone,
And heavily from woe to woe tell o'er
The sad account of fore-bemoanèd moan,
Which I new pay as if not paid before.
   But if the while I think on thee, dear friend,
   All losses are restored and sorrows end.

JAMES HENRY

Another and another and another
And still another sunset and sunrise,
The same yet different, different yet the same,
Seen by me now in my declining years
As in my early childhood, youth and manhood;
And by my parents and my parents' parents,
And by the parents of my parents' parents,
And by their parents counted back for ever,
Seen, all their lives long, even as now by me;
And by my children and my children's children
And by the children of my children's children
And by their children counted on for ever
Still to be seen as even now seen by me;
Clear and bright sometimes, sometimes dark and
    clouded
But still the same sunsetting and sunrise;
The same for ever to the never ending
Line of observers, to the same observer
Through all the changes of his life the same:
Sunsetting and sunrising and sunsetting,
And then again sunrising and sunsetting,
Sunrising and sunsetting evermore.

Intimations
of Mortality

MARK STRAND

A Morning

I have carried it with me each day: that morning I took
my uncle's boat from the brown water cove
and headed for Mosher Island.
Small waves splashed against the hull
and the hollow creak of oarlock and oar
rose into the woods of black pine crusted with lichen.
I moved like a dark star, drifting over the drowned
other half of the world until, by a distant prompting,
I looked over the gunwale and saw beneath the surface
a luminous room, a light-filled grave, saw for the first time
the one clear place given to us when we are alone.

EDMUND BLUNDEN

The Midnight Skaters

The hop-poles stand in cones,
  The icy pond lurks under,
The pole-tops steeple to the thrones
  Of stars, sound gulfs of wonder;
But not the tallest there, 'tis said,
Could fathom to this pond's black bed.

Then is not death at watch
  Within those secret waters?
What wants he but to catch
  Earth's heedless sons and daughters?
With but a crystal parapet
Between, he has his engines set.

Then on, blood shouts, on, on,
  Twirl, wheel and whip above him,
Dance on this ball-floor thin and wan,
  Use him as though you love him;
Court him, elude him, reel and pass,
And let him hate you through the glass.

EDNA ST VINCENT MILLAY

Dirge Without Music

I am not resigned to the shutting away of loving hearts in
    the hard ground.
So it is, and so it will be, for so it has been, time out of mind:
Into the darkness they go, the wise and the lovely. Crowned
With lilies and with laurel they go; but I am not resigned.

Lovers and thinkers, into the earth with you.
Be one with the dull, the indiscriminate dust.
A fragment of what you felt, of what you knew,
A formula, a phrase remains, – but the best is lost.

The answers quick and keen, the honest look, the laughter,
    the love, –
They are gone. They are gone to feed the roses. Elegant
    and curled
Is the blossom. Fragrant is the blossom. I know. But I do
    not approve.
More precious was the light in your eyes than all the roses
    in the world.

Down, down, down into the darkness of the grave
Gently they go, the beautiful, the tender, the kind;
Quietly they go, the intelligent, the witty, the brave.
I know. But I do not approve. And I am not resigned.

DYLAN THOMAS

Do not go gentle into that good night

Do not go gentle into that good night,
Old age should burn and rave at close of day;
Rage, rage against the dying of the light.

Though wise men at their end know dark is right,
Because their words had forked no lightning they
Do not go gentle into that good night.

Good men, the last wave by, crying how bright
Their frail deeds might have danced in a green bay,
Rage, rage against the dying of the light.

Wild men who caught and sang the sun in flight,
And learn, too late, they grieved it on its way,
Do not go gentle into that good night.

Grave men, near death, who see with blinding sight
Blind eyes could blaze like meteors and be gay,
Rage, rage against the dying of the light.

And you, my father, there on the sad height,
Curse, bless, me now with your fierce tears, I pray.
Do not go gentle into that good night.
Rage, rage against the dying of the light.

CHRISTOPHER MARLOWE

from *Doctor Faustus*, scene xiv

The clock strikes eleven.

FAUSTUS:

Ah, Faustus,
Now hast thou but one bare hour to live,
And then thou must be damned perpetually.
Stand still, you ever-moving spheres of heaven,
That time may cease and midnight never come!
Fair nature's eye, rise, rise again, and make
Perpetual day, or let this hour be but
A year, a month, a week, a natural day,
That Faustus may repent and save his soul!
O lente, lente currite noctis equi!
The stars move still, time runs, the clock will strike,
The devil will come, and Faustus must be damned.
O, I'll leap up to my God! Who pulls me down?
See, see where Christ's blood streams in the firmament!
One drop would save my soul, half a drop. Ah, my
    Christ!
Ah, rend not my heart for naming of my Christ!
Yet will I call on him. O, spare me, Lucifer!
Where is it now? 'Tis gone; and see where God
Stretcheth out his arm and bends his ireful brows!
Mountains and hills, come, come and fall on me,
And hide me from the heavy wrath of God!
No, no!
Then will I headlong run into the earth.
Earth, gape! O, no, it will not harbour me.
You stars that reigned at my nativity,
Whose influence hath allotted death and hell,
Now draw up Faustus like a foggy mist
Into the entrails of yon labouring cloud,
That when you vomit forth into the air,

My limbs may issue from your smoky mouths,
So that my soul may but ascend to heaven.
   The watch strikes.
Ah, half the hour is past!
'Twill all be past anon.
O God,
If thou wilt not have mercy on my soul,
Yet for Christ's sake, whose blood hath ransomed me,
Impose some end to my incessant pain.
Let Faustus live in hell a thousand years,
A hundred thousand, and at last be saved.
O, no end is limited to damnèd souls.
Why wert thou not a creature wanting soul?
Or why is this immortal that thou hast?
Ah, Pythagoras' *metempsychosis*, were that true,
This soul should fly from me and I be changed
Unto some brutish beast.
All beasts are happy, for, when they die,
Their souls are soon dissolved in elements,
But mine must live still to be plagued in hell.
Curst be the parents that engendered me!
No, Faustus, curse thyself. Curse Lucifer,
That hath deprived thee of the joys of heaven.
   The clock striketh twelve.
O, it strikes, it strikes! Now, body, turn to air,
Or Lucifer will bear thee quick to hell.
   Thunder and lightning.
O soul, be changed into little waterdrops,
And fall into the ocean, ne'er be found!
My God, my God, look not so fierce on me!
   Enter [LUCIFER, MEPHISTOPHELES, *and other*]
   DEVILS.
Adders and serpents, let me breathe a while!
Ugly hell, gape not. Come not, Lucifer!
I'll burn my books. Ah, Mephistopheles!
                [*The* DEVILS] *exeunt with him.*

WILFRED OWEN

Futility

Move him into the sun –
Gently its touch awoke him once,
At home, whispering of fields half-sown.
Always it woke him, even in France,
Until this morning and this snow.
If anything might rouse him now
The kind old sun will know.

Think how it wakes the seeds –
Woke once the clays of a cold star.
Are limbs, so dear achieved, are sides
Full-nerved, still warm, too hard to stir?
Was it for this the clay grew tall?
– O what made fatuous sunbeams toil
To break earth's sleep at all?

HENRY VAUGHAN

They are all gone into the world of light!
   And I alone sit lingring here;
Their very memory is fair and bright,
     And my sad thoughts doth clear.

It glows and glitters in my cloudy breast
   Like stars upon some gloomy grove,
Or those faint beams in which this hill is drest,
     After the Sun's remove.

I see them walking in an Air of glory,
   Whose light doth trample on my days:
My days, which are at best but dull and hoary,
     Mere glimering and decays.

O holy hope! and high humility,
   High as the Heavens above!
These are your walks, and you have shew'd them me
     To kindle my cold love,

Dear, beauteous death! the Jewel of the Just,
   Shining nowhere, but in the dark;
What mysteries do lie beyond thy dust;
     Could man outlook that mark!

He that hath found some fledg'd birds nest, may know
   At first sight, if the bird be flown;
But what fair Well, or Grove he sings in now,
     That is to him unknown.

And yet, as Angels in some brighter dreams
   Call to the soul, when man doth sleep:
So some strange thoughts transcend our wonted
     theams,
     And into glory peep.

If a star were confin'd into a Tomb
   Her captive flames must needs burn there;
But when the hand that lockt her up, gives room,
    She'll shine through all the sphære.

O Father of eternal life, and all
   Created glories under thee!
Resume thy spirit from this world of thrall
    Into true liberty.

Either disperse these mists, which blot and fill
   My perspective (still) as they pass,
Or else remove me hence unto that hill,
    Where I shall need no glass.

WALTER SAVAGE LANDOR

Age

Death, tho I see him not, is near
And grudges me my eightieth year.
Now, I would give him all these last
For one that fifty have run past.
Ah! he strikes all things, all alike,
But bargains: those he will not strike.

ALFRED, LORD TENNYSON

Tithonus

The woods decay, the woods decay and fall,
The vapours weep their burthen to the ground,
Man comes and tills the field and lies beneath,
And after many a summer dies the swan.
Me only cruel immortality
Consumes: I wither slowly in thine arms,
Here at the quiet limit of the world,
A white-hair'd shadow roaming like a dream
The ever-silent spaces of the East,
Far-folded mists, and gleaming halls of morn.

Alas! for this gray shadow, once a man –
So glorious in his beauty and thy choice,
Who madest him thy chosen, that he seem'd
To his great heart none other than a God!
I ask'd thee, 'Give me immortality.'
Then didst thou grant mine asking with a smile,
Like wealthy men, who care not how they give.
But thy strong Hours indignant work'd their wills,
And beat me down and marr'd and wasted me,
And tho' they could not end me, left me maim'd
To dwell in presence of immortal youth,
Immortal age beside immortal youth,
And all I was, in ashes. Can thy love,
Thy beauty, make amends, tho' even now,
Close over us, the silver star, thy guide,
Shines in those tremulous eyes that fill with tears
To hear me? Let me go: take back thy gift:
Why should a man desire in any way
To vary from the kindly race of men
Or pass beyond the goal of ordinance
Where all should pause, as is most meet for all?

A soft air fans the cloud apart; there comes
A glimpse of that dark world where I was born.
Once more the old mysterious glimmer steals
From thy pure brows, and from thy shoulders pure,
And bosom beating with a heart renew'd.
Thy cheek begins to redden thro' the gloom,
Thy sweet eyes brighten slowly close to mine,
Ere yet they blind the stars, and the wild team
Which love thee, yearning for thy yoke, arise,
And shake the darkness from their loosen'd manes,
And beat the twilight into flakes of fire.

    Lo! ever thus thou growest beautiful
In silence, then before thine answer given
Departest, and thy tears are on my cheek.

    Why wilt thou ever scare me with thy tears,
And make me tremble lest a saying learnt,
In days far-off, on that dark earth, be true?
'The Gods themselves cannot recall their gifts.'

    Ay me! ay me! with what another heart
In days far-off, and with what other eyes
I used to watch – if I be he that watch'd –
The lucid outline forming round thee; saw
The dim curls kindle into sunny rings;
Changed with thy mystic change, and felt my blood
Glow with the glow that slowly crimson'd all
Thy presence and thy portals, while I lay,
Mouth, forehead, eyelids, growing dewy-warm
With kisses balmier than half-opening buds
Of April, and could hear the lips that kiss'd
Whispering I knew not what of wild and sweet,
Like that strange song I heard Apollo sing,
While Ilion like a mist rose into towers.

Yet hold me not for ever in thine East:
How can my nature longer mix with thine?
Coldly thy rosy shadows bathe me, cold
Are all thy lights, and cold my wrinkled feet
Upon thy glimmering thresholds, when the steam
Floats up from those dim fields about the homes
Of happy men that have the power to die,
And grassy barrows of the happier dead.
Release me, and restore me to the ground;
Thou seëst all things, thou wilt see my grave:
Thou wilt renew thy beauty morn by morn;
I earth in earth forget these empty courts,
And thee returning on thy silver wheels.

EMILY DICKINSON

Because I could not stop for Death –
He kindly stopped for me –
The Carriage held but just Ourselves –
And Immortality.

We slowly drove – He knew no haste
And I had put away
My labor and my leisure too,
For His Civility –

We passed the School, where Children strove
At Recess – in the Ring –
We passed the Fields of Gazing Grain –
We passed the Setting Sun –

Or rather – He passed Us –
The Dews drew quivering and chill –
For only Gossamer, my Gown –
My Tippet – only Tulle –

We paused before a House that seemed
A Swelling of the Ground –
The Roof was scarcely visible –
The Cornice – in the Ground –

Since then – 'tis Centuries – and yet
Feels shorter than the Day
I first surmised the Horses' Heads
Were toward Eternity –

SIR WALTER RALEGH

A Farewell to Court

Like truthless dreams, so are my joys expired,
    And past return are all my dandled days,
My love misled, and fancy quite retired;
    Of all which past, the sorrow only stays.

My lost delights, now clean from sight of land,
    Have left me all alone in unknown ways,
My mind to woe, my life in fortune's hand;
    Of all which past, the sorrow only stays.

As in a country strange without companion,
    I only wail the wrong of death's delays,
Whose sweet spring spent, whose summer well nigh
        done;
    Of all which past, the sorrow only stays;

Whom care forewarns, ere age and winter cold,
To haste me hence to find my fortune's fold.

THOMAS CAMPION

Never weather-beaten Sail more willing bent to shore,
Never tired Pilgrim's limbs affected slumber more,
Than my wearied spright now longs to fly out of my troubled
     breast.
  O come quickly, sweetest Lord, and take my soul to rest.

Ever-blooming are the joys of Heav'n's high paradise,
Cold age deafs not there our ears, nor vapour dims our eyes:
Glory there the Sun outshines, whose beams the blessed only see;
  O come quickly, glorious Lord, and raise my spright to thee.

ALEXANDER POPE

The Dying Christian to His Soul

Vital spark of heav'nly flame!
Quit, oh quit this mortal frame:
Trembling, hoping, ling'ring, flying,
Oh the pain, the bliss of dying!
Cease, fond Nature, cease thy strife,
And let me languish into life.

Hark! they whisper; Angels say,
'Sister Spirit, come away!'
What is this absorbs me quite?
Steals my senses, shuts my sight,
Drowns my spirits, draws my breath?
Tell me, my Soul, can this be Death?

The world recedes; it disappears!
Heav'n opens on my eyes! my ears
With sounds seraphic ring:
Lend, lend your wings! I mount! I fly!
O Grave! where is thy Victory?
O Death! where is thy Sting?

JOHN DONNE

Death be not proud, though some have called thee
Mighty and dreadful, for thou art not so,
For, those, whom thou think'st thou dost overthrow,
Die not, poor death, nor yet canst thou kill me.
From rest and sleep, which but thy pictures be,
Much pleasure, then from thee, much more must flow,
And soonest our best men with thee do go,
Rest of their bones, and soul's delivery.
Thou art slave to Fate, chance, kings, and desperate men,
And dost with poison, war, and sickness dwell,
And poppy, or charms can make us sleep as well,
And better than thy stroke; why swell'st thou then?
One short sleep past, we wake eternally,
And death shall be no more; death, thou shalt die.

WILLIAM SHAKESPEARE

from *Cymbeline*, IV, ii

GUIDERIUS:
> Fear no more the heat o' the sun,
> Nor the furious winter's rages.
> Thou thy worldly task hast done,
> Home art gone and ta'en thy wages.
> Golden lads and girls all must,
> As chimney-sweepers, come to dust.

ARVIRAGUS:
> Fear no more the frown o' the great,
> Thou art past the tyrant's stroke.
> Care no more to clothe and eat,
> To thee the reed is as the oak.
> The sceptre, learning, physic, must
> All follow this and come to dust.

GUIDERIUS:
> Fear no more the lightning flash,

ARVIRAGUS:
> Nor the all-dreaded thunder-stone.

GUIDERIUS:
> Fear not slander, censure rash.

ARVIRAGUS:
> Thou hast finished joy and moan.

GUIDERIUS *and* ARVIRAGUS:
> All lovers young, all lovers must
> Consign to thee and come to dust.

GUIDERIUS:
> No exorciser harm thee,

ARVIRAGUS:
> Nor no witchcraft charm thee.

GUIDERIUS:
> Ghost unlaid forbear thee.

ARVIRAGUS:
　　Nothing ill come near thee.
GUIDERIUS *and* ARVIRAGUS:
　　Quiet consummation have,
　　And renownèd be thy grave.

EMILY BRONTË

No coward soul is mine
No trembler in the world's storm-troubled sphere
I see Heaven's glories shine
And Faith shines equal arming me from Fear

O God within my breast
Almighty ever-present Deity
Life, that in me hast rest
As I Undying Life, have power in thee

Vain are the thousand creeds
That move men's hearts, unutterably vain,
Worthless as withered weeds
Or idlest froth amid the boundless main

To waken doubt in one
Holding so fast by thy infinity
So surely anchored on
The steadfast rock of Immortality

With wide-embracing love
Thy spirit animates eternal years
Pervades and broods above,
Changes, sustains, dissolves, creates and rears

Though Earth and moon were gone
And suns and universes ceased to be
And thou wert left alone
Every Existence would exist in thee

There is not room for Death
Nor atom that his might could render void
Since thou art Being and Breath
And what thou art may never be destroyed

GEORGE ELIOT

O may I join the choir invisible
Of those immortal dead who live again
In minds made better by their presence: live
In pulses stirred to generosity,
In deeds of daring rectitude, in scorn
For miserable aims that end with self,
In thoughts sublime that pierce the night like stars,
And with their mild persistence urge man's search
To vaster issues.
        So to live is heaven:
To make undying music in the world,
Breathing as beauteous order that controls
With growing sway the growing life of man.
So we inherit that sweet purity
For which we struggled, failed, and agonised
With widening retrospect that bred despair.
Rebellious flesh that would not be subdued,
A vicious parent shaming still its child
Poor anxious penitence, is quick dissolved;
Its discords, quenched by meeting harmonies,
Die in the large and charitable air.
And all our rarer, better, truer self,
That sobbed religiously in yearning song,
That watched to ease the burthen of the world,
Laboriously tracing what must be,
And what may yet be better – saw within
A worthier image for the sanctuary,
And shaped it forth before the multitude
Divinely human, raising worship so
To higher reverence more mixed with love –
That better self shall live till human Time
Shall fold its eyelids, and the human sky
Be gathered like a scroll within the tomb
Unread for ever.

This is life to come,
Which martyred men have made more glorious
For us who strive to follow. May I reach
That purest heaven, be to other souls
The cup of strength in some great agony,
Enkindle generous ardour, feed pure love,
Beget the smiles that have no cruelty –
Be the sweet presence of a good diffused,
And in diffusion ever more intense.
So shall I join the choir invisible
Whose music is the gladness of the world.

RUPERT BROOKE

The Soldier

If I should die, think only this of me:
 That there's some corner of a foreign field
That is for ever England. There shall be
 In that rich earth a richer dust concealed;
A dust whom England bore, shaped, made aware,
 Gave, once, her flowers to love, her ways to roam,
A body of England's, breathing English air,
 Washed by the rivers, blest by suns of home.

And think, this heart, all evil shed away,
 A pulse in the eternal mind, no less
  Gives somewhere back the thoughts by England
   given;
Her sights and sounds; dreams happy as her day;
 And laughter, learnt of friends; and gentleness,
  In hearts at peace, under an English heaven.

JULIA ALVAREZ

Last Trees

When I think of my death, I think of trees
in the full of summer, a row of them
describing a border, too distant yet
for me to name them, posted with rusting boards
everyone but the faint of heart ignores.
(By then, I hope not to be one of them.)
I want to go boldly to the extreme
verge of a life I've lived to the fullest
and climb over the tumbled rocks or crawl
under the wire, never looking back –

for if I were to turn and see the house
perched on its hillside, windows flashing light,
the wash plaintive with tearful handkerchiefs,
or hear a dear voice calling from the deck,
supper's on the table – I might lose heart,
and turn back from those trees, telling myself,
tomorrow is a better day to die . . .
Behind me, the wind blowing in the leaves
in my distracted state will seem to say
something about *true love* and *letting go* –

some poster homily which I mistrust,
and which is why I break into a run,
calling out that I'm coming, *wait for me*,
thrashing and stumbling through the underbrush,
flushing out redwing blackbirds, shaking loose
seeds for next summer's weeds from their packed pods –
only to look up, breathless, and realize
I'm heading straight for those trees with no time
left to name my favorites, *arborvitae*,
maple, oak, locust, samán, willow, elm.

LOUIS MACNEICE

The Sunlight on the Garden

The sunlight on the garden
Hardens and grows cold,
We cannot cage the minute
Within its nets of gold,
When all is told
We cannot beg for pardon.

Our freedom as free lances
Advances towards its end;
The earth compels, upon it
Sonnets and birds descend;
And soon, my friend,
We shall have no time for dances.

The sky was good for flying
Defying the church bells
And every evil iron
Siren and what it tells:
The earth compels,
We are dying, Egypt, dying

And not expecting pardon,
Hardened in heart anew,
But glad to have sat under
Thunder and rain with you,
And grateful too
For sunlight on the garden.

THOMAS HARDY

Afterwards

When the Present has latched its postern behind my
    tremulous stay,
  And the May month flaps its glad green leaves like wings,
Delicate-filmed as new-spun silk, will the neighbours say,
  'He was a man who used to notice such things'?

If it be in the dusk when, like an eyelid's soundless blink,
  The dewfall-hawk comes crossing the shades to alight
Upon the wind-warped upland thorn, a gazer may think,
  'To him this must have been a familiar sight.'

If I pass during some nocturnal blackness, mothy and warm,
  When the hedgehog travels furtively over the lawn,
One may say, 'He strove that such innocent creatures should
    come to no harm,
  But he could do little for them; and now he is gone.'

If, when hearing that I have been stilled at last, they stand
    at the door,
  Watching the full-starred heavens that winter sees,
Will this thought rise on those who will meet my face no
    more,
  'He was one who had an eye for such mysteries'?

And will any say when my bell of quittance is heard in the
    gloom,
  And a crossing breeze cuts a pause in its outrollings,
Till they rise again, as they were a new bell's boom,
  'He hears it not now, but used to notice such things'?

CHRISTINA G. ROSSETTI

Remember

Remember me when I am gone away,
    Gone far away into the silent land;
    When you can no more hold me by the hand,
Nor I half turn to go yet turning stay.
Remember me when no more day by day
    You tell me of our future that you planned:
    Only remember me; you understand
It will be late to counsel then or pray.
Yet if you should forget me for a while
    And afterwards remember, do not grieve:
    For if the darkness and corruption leave
    A vestige of the thoughts that once I had,
Better by far you should forget and smile
    Than that you should remember and be sad.

D. H. LAWRENCE

Bavarian Gentians

Not every man has gentians in his house
in Soft September, at slow, Sad Michaelmas.

Bavarian gentians, big and dark, only dark
darkening the day-time torch-like with the smoking
    blueness of Pluto's gloom,
ribbed and torch-like, with their blaze of darkness
    spread blue
down flattening into points, flattened under the sweep
    of white day
torch-flower of the blue-smoking darkness, Pluto's
    dark-blue daze,
black lamps from the halls of Dio, burning dark blue,
giving off darkness, blue darkness, as Demeter's pale
    lamps give off light,
lead me then, lead me the way.

Reach me a gentian, give me a torch
let me guide myself with the blue, forked torch of this
    flower
down the darker and darker stairs, where blue is
    darkened on blueness
even where Persephone goes, just now, from the frosted
    September
to the sightless realm where darkness is awake upon the
    dark
and Persephone herself is but a voice
or a darkness invisible enfolded in the deeper dark
of the arms of Plutonic, and pierced with the passion of
    dense gloom,
among the splendour of torches of darkness, shedding
    darkness on the lost bride and her groom.

CAROLINE OLIPHANT, BARONESS NAIRNE

The Land o' the Leal

I'm wearin' awa', John,
Like snaw-wreaths in thaw, John,
I'm wearin' awa'
  To the land o' the leal.
There's nae sorrow there, John,
There's neither cauld nor care, John,
The day's aye fair
  In the land o' the leal.

Our bonnie bairn's there, John,
She was baith gude and fair, John,
And oh! we grudged her sair
  To the land o' the leal.
But sorrow's sel' wears past, John,
And joy's a-comin' fast, John,
The joy that's aye to last,
  In the land o' the leal.

Sae dear's that joy was bought, John,
Sae free the battle fought, John,
That sinfu' man e'er brought
  To the land o' the leal.
Oh! dry your glist'ning e'e, John,
My saul langs to be free, John,
And angels beckon me
  To the land o' the leal.

Leal loyal; *sair* sore

Oh! haud ye leal and true, John,
Your day it's wearin' through, John,
And I'll welcome you
    To the land o' the leal.
Now fare-ye-weel, my ain John,
This warld's cares are vain, John,
We'll meet, and we'll be fain,
    In the land o' the leal.

KATHERINE, LADY DYER

[Epitaph on Sir William Dyer]

My dearest dust could not thy hasty day
Afford thy drowsy patience leave to stay
One hour longer: so that we might either
Sit up or go to bed together?
But since thy finished labour hath possessed
Thy weary limbs with early rest,
Enjoy it sweetly; and thy widow bride
Shall soon repose her by thy slumbering side;
Whose business, now, is only to prepare
My nightly dress and call to prayer:
Mine eyes wax heavy and the day grows old.
The dew falls thick, my blood grows cold;
Draw, draw the closed curtains: and make room;
My dear, my dearest dust; I come, I come.

fain affectionate

CHARLES CAUSLEY

Eden Rock

They are waiting for me somewhere beyond Eden Rock:
My father, twenty-five, in the same suit
Of Genuine Irish Tweed, his terrier Jack
Still two years old and trembling at his feet.

My mother, twenty-three, in a sprigged dress
Drawn at the waist, ribbon in her straw hat,
Has spread the stiff white cloth over the grass.
Her hair, the colour of wheat, takes on the light.

She pours tea from a Thermos, the milk straight
From an old H.P. sauce bottle, a screw
Of paper for a cork; slowly sets out
The same three plates, the tin cups painted blue.

The sky whitens as if lit by three suns.
My mother shades her eyes and looks my way
Over the drifted stream. My father spins
A stone along the water. Leisurely,

They beckon to me from the other bank.
I hear them call, 'See where the stream-path is!
Crossing is not as hard as you might think.'

I had not thought that it would be like this.

EDMUND WALLER

Of the Last Verses in the Book

When we for Age could neither read nor write,
The Subject made us able to indite.
The Soul with Nobler Resolutions deckt,
The Body stooping, does Herself erect:
No Mortal Parts are requisite to raise
Her, that Unbody'd can her Maker praise.

The Seas are quiet, when the Winds give o're;
So calm are we, when Passions are no more:
For then we know how vain it was to boast
Of fleeting Things, so certain to be lost.
Clouds of Affection from our younger Eyes
Conceal that emptiness, which Age descries.

The Soul's dark Cottage, batter'd and decay'd,
Lets in new Light thrò chinks that time has made;
Stronger by weakness, wiser Men become
As they draw near to their Eternal home:
Leaving the Old, both Worlds at once they view,
That stand upon the Threshold of the New.

ALFRED, LORD TENNYSON

Crossing the Bar

Sunset and evening star,
   And one clear call for me!
And may there be no moaning of the bar,
   When I put out to sea,

But such a tide as moving seems asleep,
   Too full for sound and foam,
When that which drew from out the boundless deep
   Turns again home.

Twilight and evening bell,
   And after that the dark!
And may there be no sadness of farewell,
   When I embark;

For though from out our bourne of Time and Place
   The flood may bear me far,
I hope to see my Pilot face to face
   When I have crost the bar.

ALDEN NOWLAN

This is What I Wanted to Sign Off With

You know what I'm
like when I'm sick: I'd sooner
curse than cry. And people don't often
know what they're saying in the end.
Or I could die in my sleep.

So I'll say it now. Here it is.
Don't pay any attention
if I don't get it right
when it's for real. Blame that
on terror and pain
or the stuff they're shooting
into my veins. This is what I wanted to
sign off with. Bend
closer, listen, I love you.

WALTER SAVAGE LANDOR

Death stands above me, whispering low
    I know not what into my ear:
Of his strange language all I know
    Is, there is not a word of fear.

RAYMOND CARVER

Late Fragment

And did you get what
you wanted from this life, even so?
I did.
And what did you want?
To call myself beloved, to feel myself
beloved on the earth.

Mourning
and
Monuments

W. H. AUDEN

Funeral Blues

Stop all the clocks, cut off the telephone,
Prevent the dog from barking with a juicy bone,
Silence the pianos and with muffled drum
Bring out the coffin, let the mourners come.

Let aeroplanes circle moaning overhead
Scribbling on the sky the message He Is Dead,
Put crêpe bows round the white necks of the public
     doves,
Let the traffic policemen wear black cotton gloves.

He was my North, my South, my East and West,
My working week and my Sunday rest,
My noon, my midnight, my talk, my song;
I thought that love would last for ever: I was wrong.

The stars are not wanted now; put out every one,
Pack up the moon and dismantle the sun,
Pour away the ocean and sweep up the wood;
For nothing now can ever come to any good.

WILFRED OWEN

Anthem for Doomed Youth

What passing-bells for these who die as cattle?
   – Only the monstrous anger of the guns.
   Only the stuttering rifles' rapid rattle
Can patter out their hasty orisons.
No mockeries now for them; no prayers nor bells;
   Nor any voice of mourning save the choirs, –
The shrill, demented choirs of wailing shells;
   And bugles calling for them from sad shires.

What candles may be held to speed them all?
   Not in the hands of boys but in their eyes
Shall shine the holy glimmers of goodbyes.
   The pallor of girls' brows shall be their pall;
Their flowers the tenderness of patient minds,
And each slow dusk a drawing-down of blinds.

ALFRED, LORD TENNYSON

from *In Memoriam A. H. H.*

VII

Dark house, by which once more I stand
   Here in the long unlovely street,
   Doors, where my heart was used to beat
So quickly, waiting for a hand,

A hand that can be clasped no more –
   Behold me, for I cannot sleep,
   And like a guilty thing I creep
At earliest morning to the door.

He is not here; but far away
   The noise of life begins again,
   And ghastly through the drizzling rain
On the bald street breaks the blank day.

GERARD MANLEY HOPKINS

No worst, there is none. Pitched past pitch of grief,
More pangs will, schooled at forepangs, wilder wring.
Comforter, where, where is your comforting?
Mary, mother of us, where is your relief?
My cries heave, herds-long; huddle in a main, a chief
Woe, wórld-sorrow; on an áge-old anvil wince and sing –
Then lull, then leave off. Fury had shrieked 'No ling-
ering! Let me be fell: force I must be brief'.

   O the mind, mind has mountains; cliffs of fall
Frightful, sheer, no-man-fathomed. Hold them cheap
May who ne'er hung there. Nor does long our small
Durance deal with that steep or deep. Here! creep,
Wretch, under a comfort serves in a whirlwind: all
Life death does end and each day dies with sleep.

ELIZABETH BARRETT BROWNING

Grief

I tell you, hopeless grief is passionless;
That only men incredulous of despair,
Half-taught in anguish, through the midnight air
Beat upward to God's throne in loud access
Of shrieking and reproach. Full desertness,
In souls as countries, lieth silent-bare
Under the blanching, vertical eye-glare
Of the absolute Heavens. Deep-hearted man, express
Grief for thy Dead in silence like to death –
Most like a monumental statue set
In everlasting watch and moveless woe
Till itself crumble to the dust beneath.
Touch it; the marble eyelids are not wet:
If it could weep, it could arise and go.

IVOR GURNEY

To His Love

He's gone, and all our plans
    Are useless indeed.
We'll walk no more on Cotswold
    Where the sheep feed
    Quietly and take no heed.

His body that was so quick
    Is not as you
Knew it, on Severn river
    Under the blue
    Driving our small boat through.

You would not know him now . . .
    But still he died
Nobly, so cover him over
    With violets of pride
    Purple from Severn side.

Cover him, cover him soon!
    And with thick-set
Masses of memoried flowers –
    Hide that red wet
    Thing I must somehow forget.

DOUGLAS DUNN

The Kaleidoscope

To climb these stairs again, bearing a tray,
Might be to find you pillowed with your books,
Your inventories listing gowns and frocks
As if preparing for a holiday.
Or, turning from the landing, I might find
My presence watched through your kaleidoscope,
A symmetry of husbands, each redesigned
In lovely forms of foresight, prayer and hope.
I climb these stairs a dozen times a day
And, by that open door, wait, looking in
At where you died. My hands become a tray
Offering me, my flesh, my soul, my skin.
Grief wrongs us so. I stand, and wait, and cry
For the absurd forgiveness, not knowing why.

EDNA ST VINCENT MILLAY

Time does not bring relief; you all have lied
Who told me time would ease me of my pain!
I miss him in the weeping of the rain;
I want him at the shrinking of the tide;
The old snows melt from every mountain-side,
And last year's leaves are smoke in every lane;
But last year's bitter loving must remain
Heaped on my heart, and my old thoughts abide.
There are a hundred places where I fear
To go, – so with his memory they brim.
And entering with relief some quiet place
Where never fell his foot or shone his face
I say, 'There is no memory of him here!'
And so stand stricken, so remembering him.

WILLIAM WORDSWORTH

Surprized by joy – impatient as the Wind
I wished to share the transport – Oh! with whom
But Thee, long buried in the silent Tomb,
That spot which no vicissitude can find?
Love, faithful love recalled thee to my mind –
But how could I forget thee? – Through what power,
Even for the least division of an hour,
Have I been so beguiled as to be blind
To my most grievous loss? – That thought's return
Was the worst pang that sorrow ever bore,
Save one, one only, when I stood forlorn,
Knowing my heart's best treasure was no more;
That neither present time, nor years unborn
Could to my sight that heavenly face restore.

THOMAS HARDY

After a Journey

Hereto I come to view a voiceless ghost;
   Whither, O whither will its whim now draw me?
Up the cliff, down, till I'm lonely, lost,
   And the unseen waters' ejaculations awe me.
Where you will next be there's no knowing,
   Facing round about me everywhere,
      With your nut-coloured hair,
And gray eyes, and rose-flush coming and going.

Yes: I have re-entered your olden haunts at last;
   Through the years, through the dead scenes I have
        tracked you;
What have you now found to say of our past –
   Scanned across the dark space wherein I have
        lacked you?
Summer gave us sweets, but autumn wrought division?
   Things were not lastly as firstly well
      With us twain, you tell?
But all's closed now, despite Time's derision.

I see what you are doing: you are leading me on
   To the spots we knew when we haunted here
        together,
The waterfall, above which the mist-bow shone
   At the then fair hour in the then fair weather,
And the cave just under, with a voice still so hollow
   That it seems to call out to me from forty years ago,
      When you were all aglow,
And not the thin ghost that I now fraily follow!

Ignorant of what there is flitting here to see,
    The waked birds preen and the seals flop lazily;
Soon you will have, Dear, to vanish from me,
    For the stars close their shutters and the dawn whitens
        hazily.
Trust me, I mind not, though Life lours,
    The bringing me here; nay, bring me here again!
        I am just the same as when
Our days were a joy, and our paths through flowers.

ANONYMOUS (15TH CENTURY)

The Unquiet Grave

The wind doth blow today, my love,
And a few small drops of rain;
I never had but one true-love,
In cold grave she was lain.

I'll do as much for my true-love
As any young man may;
I'll sit and mourn all at her grave
For a twelvemonth and a day.

The twelvemonth and a day being up,
The dead began to speak:
'Oh who sits weeping on my grave,
And will not let me sleep?'

'Tis I, my love, sits on your grave,
And will not let you sleep;
For I crave one kiss of your clay-cold lips,
And that is all I seek.

'You crave one kiss of my clay-cold lips;
But my breath smells earthy strong;
If you have one kiss of my clay-cold lips,
Your time will not be long.

' 'Tis down in yonder garden green,
Love, where we used to walk,
The finest flower that ere was seen
Is withered to a stalk.

'The stalk is withered dry, my love,
So will our hearts decay;
So make yourself content, my love,
Till God calls you away.'

EMILY BRONTË

Remembrance

Cold in the earth – and the deep snow piled above thee,
Far, far, removed, cold in the dreary grave!
Have I forgot, my only Love, to love thee,
Severed at last by Time's all-severing wave?

Now, when alone, do my thoughts no longer hover
Over the mountains, on that northern shore,
Resting their wings where heath and fern-leaves cover
Thy noble heart for ever, ever more?

Cold in the earth – and fifteen wild Decembers,
From those brown hills, have melted into spring:
Faithful, indeed, is the spirit that remembers
After such years of change and suffering!

Sweet Love of youth, forgive, if I forget thee,
While the world's tide is bearing me along;
Other desires and other hopes beset me,
Hopes which obscure, but cannot do thee wrong!

No later light has lightened up my heaven,
No second morn has ever shone for me;
All my life's bliss from thy dear life was given,
All my life's bliss is in the grave with thee.

But, when the days of golden dreams had perished,
And even Despair was powerless to destroy;
Then did I learn how existence could be cherished,
Strengthened, and fed without the aid of joy.

Then did I check the tears of useless passion –
Weaned my young soul from yearning after thine;
Sternly denied its burning wish to hasten
Down to that tomb already more than mine.

And, even yet, I dare not let it languish,
Dare not indulge in memory's rapturous pain;
Once drinking deep of that divinest anguish,
How could I seek the empty world again?

R. S. THOMAS

Comparisons

To all light things
I compared her; to
a snowflake, a feather.

I remember she rested
at the dance on my
arm, as a bird

on its nest lest
the eggs break, lest
she lean too heavily

on our love. Snow
melts, feathers
are blown away;

I have let
her ashes down
in me like an anchor.

EMILY DICKINSON

After great pain, a formal feeling comes –
The Nerves sit ceremonious, like Tombs –
The stiff Heart questions was it He, that bore,
And Yesterday, or Centuries before?

The Feet, mechanical, go round –
Of Ground, or Air, or Ought –
A Wooden way
Regardless grown,
A Quartz contentment, like a stone –

This is the Hour of Lead –
Remembered, if outlived,
As Freezing persons, recollect the Snow –
First – Chill – then Stupor – then the letting go –

THOM GUNN

The Reassurance

About ten days or so
After we saw you dead
You came back in a dream.
I'm all right now you said.

And it *was* you, although
You were fleshed out again:
You hugged us all round then,
And gave your welcoming beam.

How like you to be kind,
Seeking to reassure.
And, yes, how like my mind
To make itself secure.

ALFRED, LORD TENNYSON

from *In Memoriam A. H. H.*

I envy not in any moods
  The captive void of noble rage,
  The linnet born within the cage,
That never knew the summer woods:

I envy not the beast that takes
  His license in the field of time,
  Unfettered by the sense of crime,
To whom a conscience never wakes;

Nor, what may count itself as blest,
  The heart that never plighted troth
  But stagnates in the weeds of sloth;
Nor any want-begotten rest.

I hold it true, whate'er befall;
  I feel it, when I sorrow most;
  'Tis better to have loved and lost
Than never to have loved at all.

WILLIAM JOHNSON CORY

Heraclitus

They told me, Heraclitus, they told me you were dead,
They brought me bitter news to hear and bitter tears to
    shed.
I wept, as I remembered, how often you and I
Had tired the sun with talking and sent him down the sky.

And now that thou art lying, my dear old Carian guest,
A handful of grey ashes, long long ago at rest,
Still are thy pleasant voices, thy nightingales, awake;
For Death, he taketh all away, but them he cannot take.

DYLAN THOMAS

And death shall have no dominion

And death shall have no dominion.
Dead men naked they shall be one
With the man in the wind and the west moon;
When their bones are picked clean and the clean bones
    gone,
They shall have stars at elbow and foot;
Though they go mad they shall be sane,
Though they sink through the sea they shall rise again;
Though lovers be lost love shall not;
And death shall have no dominion.

And death shall have no dominion.
Under the windings of the sea
They lying long shall not die windily;
Twisting on racks when sinews give way,
Strapped to a wheel, yet they shall not break;
Faith in their hands shall snap in two,
And the unicorn evils run them through;
Split all ends up they shan't crack;
And death shall have no dominion.

And death shall have no dominion.
No more may gulls cry at their ears
Or waves break loud on the seashores;
Where blew a flower may a flower no more
Lift its head to the blows of the rain;
Though they be mad and dead as nails,
Heads of the characters hammer through daisies;
Break in the sun till the sun breaks down,
And death shall have no dominion.

PERCY BYSSHE SHELLEY

from *Adonais*

Peace, peace! he is not dead, he doth not sleep –
He hath awakened from the dream of life –
'Tis we, who lost in stormy visions, keep
With phantoms an unprofitable strife,
And in mad trance, strike with our spirit's knife
Invulnerable nothings. – *We* decay
Like corpses in a charnel; fear and grief
Convulse us and consume us day by day,
And cold hopes swarm like worms within our living clay.

He has outsoared the shadow of our night;
Envy and calumny and hate and pain,
And that unrest which men miscall delight,
Can touch him not and torture not again;
From the contagion of the world's slow stain
He is secure, and now can never mourn
A heart grown cold, a head grown gray in vain;
Nor, when the spirit's self has ceased to burn,
With sparkless ashes load an unlamented urn.

ROBERT BROWNING

My Last Duchess

Ferrara

That's my last Duchess painted on the wall,
Looking as if she were alive. I call
That piece a wonder, now: Frà Pandolf's hands
Worked busily a day, and there she stands.
Will't please you sit and look at her? I said
'Frà Pandolf' by design, for never read
Strangers like you that pictured countenance,
The depth and passion of its earnest glance,
But to myself they turned (since none puts by
The curtain I have drawn for you, but I)
And seemed as they would ask me, if they durst,
How such a glance came there; so, not the first
Are you to turn and ask thus. Sir, 'twas not
Her husband's presence only, called that spot
Of joy into the Duchess' cheek: perhaps
Frà Pandolf chanced to say 'Her mantle laps
Over my lady's wrist too much,' or 'Paint
Must never hope to reproduce the faint
Half-flush that dies along her throat': such stuff
Was courtesy, she thought, and cause enough
For calling up that spot of joy. She had
A heart – how shall I say? – too soon made glad,
Too easily impressed; she liked whate'er
She looked on, and her looks went everywhere.
Sir, 'twas all one! My favour at her breast,
The dropping of the daylight in the West,
The bough of cherries some officious fool
Broke in the orchard for her, the white mule
She rode with round the terrace – all and each
Would draw from her alike the approving speech,

Or blush, at least. She thanked men, – good! but
    thanked
Somehow – I know not how – as if she ranked
My gift of a nine-hundred-years-old name
With anybody's gift. Who'd stoop to blame
This sort of trifling? Even had you skill
In speech – (which I have not) – to make your will
Quite clear to such an one, and say, 'Just this
Or that in you disgusts me; here you miss,
Or there exceed the mark' – and if she let
Herself be lessoned so, nor plainly set
Her wits to yours, forsooth, and made excuse,
– E'en then would be some stooping; and I choose
Never to stoop. Oh sir, she smiled, no doubt,
Whene'er I passed her; but who passed without
Much the same smile? This grew; I gave commands;
Then all smiles stopped together. There she stands
As if alive. Will't please you rise? We'll meet
The company below, then. I repeat,
The Count your master's known munificence
Is ample warrant that no just pretence
Of mine for dowry will be disallowed;
Though his fair daughter's self, as I avowed
At starting, is my object. Nay, we'll go
Together down, sir. Notice Neptune, though,
Taming a sea-horse, thought a rarity,
Which Claus of Innsbruck cast in bronze for me!

EZRA POUND

Epitaphs

FU I

Fu I loved the high cloud and the hill,
Alas, he died of alcohol.

LI PO

And Li Po also died drunk.
He tried to embrace a moon
In the Yellow River.

WALLACE STEVENS

A Postcard from the Volcano

Children picking up our bones
Will never know that these were once
As quick as foxes on the hill;

And that in autumn, when the grapes
Made sharp air sharper by their smell
These had a being, breathing frost;

And least will guess that with our bones
We left much more, left what still is
The look of things, left what we felt

At what we saw. The spring clouds blow
Above the shuttered mansion-house,
Beyond our gate and the windy sky

Cries out a literate despair.
We knew for long the mansion's look
And what we said of it became

A part of what it is . . . Children,
Still weaving budded aureoles,
Will speak our speech and never know,

Will say of the mansion that it seems
As if he that lived there left behind
A spirit storming in blank walls,

A dirty house in a gutted world,
A tatter of shadows peaked to white,
Smeared with the gold of the opulent sun.

PERCY BYSSHE SHELLEY

Ozymandias

I met a traveller from an antique land
Who said: 'Two vast and trunkless legs of stone
Stand in the desert. Near them, on the sand,
Half sunk, a shattered visage lies, whose frown,
And wrinkled lip, and sneer of cold command,
Tell that its sculptor well those passions read
Which yet survive, stamped on these lifeless things,
The hand that mocked them and the heart that fed;
And on the pedestal these words appear:
"My name is Ozymandias, king of kings:
Look on my works, ye Mighty, and despair!"
Nothing beside remains. Round the decay
Of that colossal wreck, boundless and bare
The lone and level sands stretch far away.'

THOMAS GRAY

Elegy Written in a Country Church Yard

The Curfew tolls the knell of parting day,
The lowing herd wind slowly o'er the lea,
The plowman homeward plods his weary way,
And leaves the world to darkness and to me.

Now fades the glimmering landscape on the sight,
And all the air a solemn stillness holds,
Save where the beetle wheels his droning flight,
And drowsy tinklings lull the distant folds;

Save that from yonder ivy-mantled tow'r
The mopeing owl does to the moon complain
Of such, as wand'ring near her secret bow'r,
Molest her ancient solitary reign.

Beneath those rugged elms, that yew-tree's shade,
Where heaves the turf in many a mould'ring heap,
Each in his narrow cell for ever laid,
The rude Forefathers of the hamlet sleep.

The breezy call of incense-breathing Morn,
The swallow twitt'ring from the straw-built shed,
The cock's shrill clarion, or the echoing horn,
No more shall rouse them from their lowly bed.

For them no more the blazing hearth shall burn,
Or busy housewife ply her evening care:
No children run to lisp their sire's return,
Or climb his knees the envied kiss to share.

Oft did the harvest to their sickle yield,
Their furrow oft the stubborn glebe has broke;
How jocund did they drive their team afield!
How bow'd the woods beneath their sturdy stroke!

Let not Ambition mock their useful toil,
Their homely joys, and destiny obscure;
Nor Grandeur hear with a disdainful smile,
The short and simple annals of the poor.

The boast of heraldry, the pomp of pow'r,
And all that beauty, all that wealth e'er gave,
Awaits alike th' inevitable hour.
The paths of glory lead but to the grave.

Nor you, ye Proud, impute to These the fault,
If Mem'ry o'er their Tomb no Trophies raise,
Where thro' the long-drawn isle and fretted vault
The pealing anthem swells the note of praise.

Can storied urn or animated bust
Back to its mansion call the fleeting breath?
Can Honour's voice provoke the silent dust,
Or Flatt'ry sooth the dull cold ear of Death?

Perhaps in this neglected spot is laid
Some heart once pregnant with celestial fire,
Hands, that the rod of empire might have sway'd,
Or wak'd to ecstasy the living lyre.

But Knowledge to their eyes her ample page
Rich with the spoils of time did ne'er unroll;
Chill Penury repress'd their noble rage,
And froze the genial current of the soul.

Full many a gem of purest ray serene,
The dark unfathom'd caves of ocean bear:
Full many a flower is born to blush unseen,
And waste its sweetness on the desert air.

Some village-Hampden, that with dauntless breast
The little Tyrant of his fields withstood;
Some mute inglorious Milton here may rest,
Some Cromwell guiltless of his country's blood.

Th' applause of list'ning senates to command,
The threats of pain and ruin to despise,
To scatter plenty o'er a smiling land,
And read their hist'ry in a nation's eyes

Their lot forbad: nor circumscrib'd alone
Their growing virtues, but their crimes confin'd;
Forbad to wade through slaughter to a throne,
And shut the gates of mercy on mankind,

The struggling pangs of conscious truth to hide,
To quench the blushes of ingenuous shame,
Or heap the shrine of Luxury and Pride
With incense kindled at the Muse's flame.

Far from the madding crowd's ignoble strife,
Their sober wishes never learn'd to stray;
Along the cool sequester'd vale of life
They kept the noiseless tenor of their way.

Yet ev'n these bones from insult to protect
Some frail memorial still erected nigh,
With uncouth rhimes and shapeless sculpture deck'd,
Implores the passing tribute of a sigh.

Their name, their years, spelt by th' unletter'd muse,
The place of fame and elegy supply:
And many a holy text around she strews,
That teach the rustic moralist to die.

For who to dumb Forgetfulness a prey,
This pleasing anxious being e'er resign'd,
Left the warm precincts of the cheerful day,
Nor cast one longing ling'ring look behind?

On some fond breast the parting soul relies,
Some pious drops the closing eye requires;
Ev'n from the tomb the voice of Nature cries,
Ev'n in our Ashes live their wonted Fires.

For thee, who mindful of th' unhonour'd Dead
Dost in these lines their artless tale relate;
If chance, by lonely contemplation led,
Some kindred Spirit shall inquire thy fate,

Haply some hoary-headed Swain may say,
'Oft have we seen him at the peep of dawn
'Brushing with hasty steps the dews away
'To meet the sun upon the upland lawn.

'There at the foot of yonder nodding beech
'That wreathes its old fantastic roots so high,
'His listless length at noontide wou'd he stretch,
'And pore upon the brook that babbles by.

'Hard by yon wood, now smiling as in scorn,
'Mutt'ring his wayward fancies he wou'd rove,
'Now drooping, woeful wan, like one forlorn,
'Or craz'd with care, or cross'd in hopeless love.

'One morn I miss'd him on the custom'd hill,
'Along the heath and near his fav'rite tree;
'Another came; nor yet beside the rill,
'Nor up the lawn, nor at the wood was he;

'The next with dirges due in sad array
'Slow thro' the church-way path we saw him borne.
'Approach and read (for thou can'st read) the lay,
'Grav'd on the stone beneath yon aged thorn.'

The Epitaph

Here rests his head upon the lap of Earth
A Youth to Fortune and to Fame unknown,
Fair Science frown'd not on his humble birth,
And Melancholy mark'd him for her own.

Large was his bounty, and his soul sincere,
Heav'n did a recompence as largely send:
He gave to Mis'ry all he had, a tear,
He gain'd from Heav'n ('twas all he wish'd) a friend.

No farther seek his merits to disclose,
Or draw his frailties from their dread abode,
(There they alike in trembling hope repose)
The bosom of his Father and his God.

STEPHEN SPENDER

I think continually of those who were truly great.
Who, from the womb, remembered the soul's history
Through corridors of light where the hours are suns,
Endless and singing. Whose lovely ambition
Was that their lips, still touched with fire,
Should tell of the Spirit, clothed from head to foot in song.
And who hoarded from the Spring branches
The desires falling across their bodies like blossoms.

What is precious, is never to forget
The essential delight of the blood drawn from ageless
      springs
Breaking through rocks in worlds before our earth.
Never to deny its pleasure in the morning simple light
Nor its grave evening demand for love.
Never to allow gradually the traffic to smother
With noise and fog, the flowering of the Spirit.

Near the snow, near the sun, in the highest fields,
See how these names are fêted by the waving grass
And by the streamers of white cloud
And whispers of wind in the listening sky.
The names of those who in their lives fought for life,
Who wore at their hearts the fire's centre.
Born of the sun, they travelled a short while toward the sun
And left the vivid air signed with their honour.

THOMAS HARDY

Transformations

Portion of this yew
Is a man my grandsire knew,
Bosomed here at its foot:
This branch may be his wife,
A ruddy human life
Now turned to a green shoot.

These grasses must be made
Of her who often prayed,
Last century, for repose;
And the fair girl long ago
Whom I often tried to know
May be entering this rose.

So, they are not underground,
But as nerves and veins abound
In the growths of upper air,
And they feel the sun and rain,
And the energy again
That made them what they were!

WALT WHITMAN

from *Song of Myself*

A child said, What is the grass? fetching it to me with full
　　hands;
How could I answer the child? . . . I do not know what it is
　　any more than he.

I guess it must be the flag of my disposition, out of hopeful
　　green stuff woven.

Or I guess it is the handkerchief of the Lord,
A scented gift and remembrancer designedly dropped,
Bearing the owner's name someway in the corners, that we
　　may see and remark, and say Whose?

Or I guess the grass is itself a child . . . the produced babe of
　　the vegetation.

Or I guess it is a uniform hieroglyphic,
And it means, Sprouting alike in broad zones and narrow
　　zones,
Growing among black folks as among white,
Kanuck, Tuckahoe, Congressman, Cuff, I give them the same,
　　I receive them the same.

And now it seems to me the beautiful uncut hair of graves.
Tenderly will I use you curling grass,
It may be you transpire from the breasts of young men,
It may be if I had known them I would have loved them;
It may be you are from old people and from women, and
　　from offspring taken soon out of their mothers' laps,
And here you are the mothers' laps.

This grass is very dark to be from the white heads of old
    mothers,
Darker than the colorless beards of old men,
Dark to come from under the faint red roofs of mouths.

O I perceive after all so many uttering tongues!
And I perceive they do not come from the roofs of mouths
    for nothing.

I wish I could translate the hints about the dead young men
    and women,
And the hints about old men and mothers, and the offspring
    soon out of their laps.

What do you think has become of the young and old men?
And what do you think has become of the women and
    children?

They are alive and well somewhere;
The smallest sprout shows there is really no death,
And if ever there was it led forward life, and does not wait
    at the end to arrest it,
And ceased the moment life appeared.

All goes onward and outward . . . and nothing collapses,
And to die is different from what any one supposed, and
    luckier.

PHILIP LARKIN

An Arundel Tomb

Side by side, their faces blurred,
The earl and countess lie in stone,
Their proper habits vaguely shown
As jointed armour, stiffened pleat,
And that faint hint of the absurd –
The little dogs under their feet.

Such plainness of the pre-baroque
Hardly involves the eye, until
It meets his left-hand gauntlet, still
Clasped empty in the other; and
One sees, with a sharp tender shock,
His hand withdrawn, holding her hand.

They would not think to lie so long.
Such faithfulness in effigy
Was just a detail friends would see:
A sculptor's sweet commissioned grace
Thrown off in helping to prolong
The Latin names around the base.

They would not guess how early in
Their supine stationary voyage
The air would change to soundless damage,
Turn the old tenantry away;
How soon succeeding eyes begin
To look, not read. Rigidly they

Persisted, linked, through lengths and breadths
Of time. Snow fell, undated. Light
Each summer thronged the glass. A bright
Litter of birdcalls strewed the same
Bone-riddled ground. And up the paths
The endless altered people came,

Washing at their identity.
Now, helpless in the hollow of
An unarmorial age, a trough
Of smoke in slow suspended skeins
Above their scrap of history,
Only an attitude remains:

Time has transfigured them into
Untruth. The stone fidelity
They hardly meant has come to be
Their final blazon, and to prove
Our almost-instinct almost true:
What will survive of us is love.

EDWIN MORGAN

Message Clear

```
    am              i
                           if
i am                    he
      he r       o
      h    ur  t
      the re          and
      he    re    and
      he re
    a               n   d
      the r               e
i am    r               ife
                i n
            s    ion and
i                   d   i e
    am  e res  ect  .
    am  e res  ection
                      o        f
      the               life
                  o        f
      m   e         n
          sur e
      the               d   i e
i         s
              s   e t   and
i am the  sur           d
  a   t   res   t
                  o            life
i am he r                   e
i a       ct
i     r   u   n
i m e e    t
i         t                 i e
i         s   t   and
```

```
i am th          o      th
i am     r           a
i am the  su      n
i am the  s      on
i am the  e   rect on      e if
i am    re      n    t
i am      s      a          fe
i am      s    e    n      t
i    he  e            d
i    t  e   s      t
i      re          a  d
 a  th  re          a  d
 a      s    t on       e
 a  t  re          a  d
 a  th  r      on       e
i          resurrect
                    a        life
i am              i  n          life
i am     resurrection
i am the resurrection and
i am
i am the resurrection and the life
```

Acknowledgements

I am very grateful to the following for conversations and correspondence about poetry, as well as for suggestions, support and wise advice: Ellah Allfrey, Rosamund Bartlett, Mariateresa Boffo, Diane Bourke, Stephen Brown, William Fiennes, Adam Freudenheim, Elizabeth Iveson, Kevin Jackson, Philip Gwyn Jones, Paul Keegan, Florence Knapp, Hilary Laurie, Arvind Krishna Mehrotra, Pankaj Mishra, Parashkev Nachev, Adriana Natcheva, Ron Pretty, Christopher Ricks, Michal Shavit, and most especially Olivia McCannon.

I dedicate this volume to my parents, John and Susan Barber, who encouraged in me a love of poetry from 'Pat-a-cake pat-a-cake' onwards.

LB

The editor and publishers gratefully acknowledge permission to reprint copyright material in this book as follows:

CHINUA ACHEBE: 'Generation Gap' from *Collected Poems*. By permission of David Higham Associates.

FLEUR ADCOCK: 'For a Five-year-old' and 'Against Coupling' from *Poems 1960–2000* (Bloodaxe Books, 2000). Reprinted by permission of the publisher.

KIM ADDONIZIO: 'For Desire' from *Tell Me*. Copyright © 2000 by Kim Addonizio. Reprinted with the permission of BOA Editions Ltd, www.boaeditions.org

PATIENCE AGBABI: 'North(west)ern' was commissioned by BBC Radio 4 for National Poetry Day 2000 and broadcast in The Windrose and first published in *Here to Eternity: An Anthology of Poetry*, edited by Andrew Motion (Faber and Faber, 2000). 'Accidentally Falling' from *R.A.W.* by Patience Agbabi (Gecko Press, 1995). Reproduced by kind permission of the author.

JULIA ALVAREZ: 'Last Trees' copyright © 1998 by Julia Alvarez. From

DICK DAVIS: 'Uxor Vivamus . . .' is taken from *Devices and Desires: New and Selected Poems 1967–1987* by Dick Davis. Published by Anvil Press Poetry in 1989. By permission of the publisher.

C. DAY LEWIS: 'Walking Away' from *Collected Poems of C. Day Lewis* (Copyright © The Estate of C. Day Lewis 1992) is reprinted by permission of PFD (www.pfd.co.uk) on behalf of the Estate of C. Day Lewis.

WALTER DE LA MARE: 'The Birthnight' from *Selected Poems* (Faber and Faber, 1973), reprinted by permission of the Literary Trustees of Walter de la Mare, and the Society of Authors as their representative.

EMILY DICKINSON: 'Wild Nights – Wild Nights!', 'Because I could not stop for Death –' and 'After great pain, a formal feeling comes –' reprinted by permission of the publishers and the Trustees of Amherst College from *The Poems of Emily Dickinson*, Thomas H. Johnson, ed., Cambridge, Mass.: The Belknap Press of Harvard University Press, Copyright © 1951, 1955, 1979, 1983 by the President and Fellows of Harvard College.

MAURA DOOLEY: 'Freight' from *Sound Barrier: Poems 1982–2002* (Bloodaxe Books, 2002). Reprinted by permission of the publisher.

CAROL ANN DUFFY: 'In Mrs Tilscher's Class' from *The Other Country* (Anvil Press Poetry, 1990) by permission of the publisher. Copyright © Carol Ann Duffy; 'Mrs Sisyphus' from *The World's Wife* (Picador, 2000) and 'White Writing' from *Feminine Gospels* (Picador, 2003) by kind permission of the author c/o Rogers, Coleridge & White Ltd, 20 Powis Mews, London W11 1JN.

SASHA DUGDALE: 'First Love' from *Notebook* (2003) by permission of Carcanet Press Limited.

DOUGLAS DUNN: 'Kaleidoscope' from *Elegies* (Faber and Faber, 2001) and 'Modern Love' from *New Selected Poems* (Faber and Faber, 2003) by permission of the publisher.

T. S. ELIOT: 'The Love-Song of J. Alfred Prufrock' from *Collected Poems and Plays* (Faber and Faber, 2004) by permission of the publisher.

ALISON FELL: 'Pushing forty' first published in *Kisses for Mayakovsky* by Alison Fell (Virago Press, 1984) and reprinted by kind permission of Peake Associates, www.tonypeake.com

ROBERT FROST: 'The Road Not Taken' from *The Poetry of Robert Frost*, ed. Edward Connery Lathem, published by Jonathan Cape and reprinted by permission of The Random House Group Ltd. And copyright 1969 by Henry Holt and Company and reprinted by permission of Henry Holt and Company, LLC.

ROBERT GRAVES: 'Warning to Children' and 'Love Without Hope' from *Complete Poems in One Volume*, edited by Patrick Quinn (2000), by permission of Carcanet Press.

Index of Poets

Index of Titles and First Lines